THE SUPREME SELF

A Modern Upanishad

Swami Abhayananda

ATMA BOOKS

Fallsburg, N. Y.

First Edition

Copyright © 1984 Swami Abhayananda

Library of Congress Cataloging in Publication Data

Abhayananda, Swami, 1938-
    The supreme Self.

    Bibliography: p.
    Includes index.
    1. Mysticism.   I. Title.
BL625.A3   1984   291.4'2   83-72702
ISBN 0-914557-01-7

Printed in the United States of America

1 2 3 4 5 6 7 8 9 10

Cover photo: *Nataraj*, early Chola, 10th century A.D.
            Victoria and Albert Museum, So. Kensington.

Cover art by Nancy Dougherty

In Thy Praise
And To Thy Glory

CONTENTS

PART FOUR: THE PSYCHOLOGY OF UNITY

PART FIVE: THE WORSHIP OF UNITY

ABOUT THIS BOOK

This book is intended to serve as an introduction to the knowledge of God, the Supreme Self. It is the attainment of this knowledge which has revolutionized the lives of the great religious teachers throughout history; and it is this very knowledge which constitutes the one common thread that binds together in unity all the great religious and philosophical traditions which have existed since time began. And yet today, though many thousands of extremely intelligent and devout men and women throughout history have experienced the direct knowledge of the Supreme Self, the vast majority of human beings in the world are either unaware that such knowledge is possible, or are indifferent to it. That the truth of existence *is* experienceable, that the mystery of God and the universe is penetrable and subject to certainty, is not so well-known as it should be, it seems to me. Nor is it so fully acknowledged as it ought to be that this universally experienced "mystical vision" is a reliable source of knowledge, applicable to a concise formulation of the nature of reality.

In order to remedy this situation, I have attempted, in this book, to explain the knowledge of the Self in a manner so thorough and satisfactory that it leaves no room for doubt or dispute. I have examined the mystical theologies of every major religious tradition and shown that, aside from the difference in regional terminologies, they are identical. I have also carefully examined the views of contemporary physicists, whose discoveries during the past century have had so profound a bearing on our understanding of the nature of

x.

reality; and I have shown that the great gap that
once existed between the world-view of science
and that of mysticism is gone -- that, in fact,
the time is not far distant when it must be universally acknowledged that these two disciplines,
though methodologically divergent, are in complete
agreement.

Having drawn from a wide variety of sources --
mystics, philosophers, physicists and saints, I
have presented the knowledge of the Supreme
Self from many different viewpoints, including
my own personal, subjective, one, in order to
provide a broad comprehensive look at this ancient
yet ever-new knowledge with its many facinating
implications. It is my hope that, for some at
least, this book will open a door of understanding
through which a ray of light may shine upon the
eternal verities.

S.A.
June, 1983

ACKNOWLEDGEMENTS

I wish to express my sincere gratitude to:
Rom Landau and George Allen & Unwin of London
for permission to reprint extracts from *The
Philosophy Of Ibn Arabi*; David Bohm, Basil
Hiley and *Foundations Of Physics* magazine for
permission to quote from the article, *"On The
Intuitive Understanding Of Non-Locality As Implied
By Quantum Theory"*; and William de Barry and
Columbia University Press for permission to
reprint the poem of Dara Shikoh from *Sources
Of Indian Tradition*.

In addition, I would like to express a special
thanks to Anne Hamilton-Byrne, without whose
unselfish generosity and warm hospitality this
book would not have been possible.

ONE

The Experience Of Unity

"The knower of Brahman becomes Brahman."

-- *Mundaka Upanishad*

I.   AWAKENING

Everyone has a spiritual awakening somewhere along the way. For me it was sudden and
unexpected. It was 1966. I was twenty-eight,
and it was a very special time in my world.
Laura and I had moved to Los Gatos, California,
in the mountains south of San Jose; we had a
beautiful house with a knotty-pine interior and
a huge porch overlooking a bubbling brook. I
worked nearby at the Post Office on a split-shift
that gave me time in the afternoons to sit on my
beautiful private porch and drink coffee and read,
or work on the great American novel I was writing.
In June of 1966, I was facinated with the
symbology of Myths, and was reading Carl Jung
and Joseph Campbell, both of whom were speaking
repeatedly about 'Vedanta', the mysterious philosophy of India. And so, when I saw in a local
bookstore a copy of *Vedanta For The Western
World*, I bought a copy. This book, edited by
Christopher Isherwood, consisted of a series of
articles by such figures as Swami Prabhavananda
and Aldous Huxley, and spelled out in very easy-
to-understand terms the philosophy of Vedanta.
Vedanta, I soon learned, refers to the
philosophy expressed in the *Upanishads*, considered to be the final appendages to the *Vedas*.
It is a non-dualistic philosophy; that is so say,
a monistic one. It admits to an *apparent* duality
between God and the world, between Consciousness
and matter, but this duality, says Vedanta, is
apparent only; in the "mystical vision" they are
experienced as one.
According to Vedanta, when a person realizes

3

God, he experiences a unity, wherein everything is seen to be a manifestation of one universal Self; he knows: "I and the Father are one." This, says Vedanta, is the perennial teaching of all the sages and saints of all times. For the experience of unity, whether called "samadhi", "satori", or "union with God", is the same for all, and is the basis for all the various religions.

Reading of this, I suddenly understood what the religious mystics had been talking about. Everything I had ever puzzled over became clear; everything fell into place. I had scarcely finished with the Introduction to this book, and I knew that I had acquired a new and profound vision which brought everything together for me and answered all my questions forever. I knew my life would never be the same. I knew I had found the key to an extraordinary wealth of understanding about myself and the nature of reality.

As I continued reading this amazing book, I was introduced to the 19th century mystic, Ramakrishna, who was mad with fervor for the mystical experience of the Self from an early age, and who became so one-pointed in mind through devotional love that he became entirely lost to the world of forms, aware only of the all-pervasive Reality. Reading of the life of Ramakrishna and other such 'saints', I felt I had entered into an elite society of delerious madmen, madmen who called themselves, 'The Lovers Of God'; who, turning away from the normal transitory pursuits of man, sought to become intimate with the very fountainhead of the universe. Reading the inspiring words of Ramakrishna, I experienced a wave of such happiness that I could scarcely bear it. Sitting on my porch, hearing these things for the first time, I experienced a shower of golden

light pouring down upon me, as though raining
on the back of my neck, and awaking a deep and
delicious chill in my body that ran up my spine
and caused my scalp to tingle.

For the first time, I understood what drew
men to religion. I had previously attributed
it to weakness of mind. How much grander was
the heritage of man than I had supposed. I had
viewed all this talk of 'God' through the ages
as the superstitious babbling of fools. But I
had been the fool. There *was* a God -- but it
was not what I had supposed men meant by the
term. "God" meant not some ethereal being with
a white beard, etc.; God was Being itself --
Existence. And the proof of it was that It could
be experienced, actually realized, seen with
the inner eye of unleashed awareness. For the
first time, I could fathom it; I understood the
method in the madness of the saints. My mind
was dazzled, ecstatic.

I was really extraordinarily happy. Of
course, all my friends thought I had gone suddenly mad. Their faces betrayed their uneasi-
ness when I began talking about 'God' and the
mystics who had known Him. I began to realize
I had touched on something that not everyone
could, or was willing to, understand. I read
about 'Grace', the amazing descent of Grace.
Such a thing seemed to be happening to me. By
some process of awakening, to which I was an
unwitting spectator, I was seeing with an
entirely new and different pair of eyes. My old
friends were unable to understand or to share
in any way the intensity of my fervor. I realized
that I would have to go on this journey alone.

Within only a few days, my life had taken
a startling and unalterable turn. I sent a note
to my employer stating that I would not be in
on Monday ... "for reasons beyond my control",
gave what I owned to Laura, and went off into

the mountains of Santa Cruz, into solitude.

How romantic it was! I was a saint Francis.
I was Rumi, the Sufi poet. I was Basho, the
Zen hermit. Walking on the country roads in
the early morning with my brown bag on my
shoulder, I'd sit myself down in the grass by
the roadside and write Zen poems to the poppies
in the fields, or to the cottontails that suddenly
went hopping through the dewy morning grass.
Walking along, the curving road would suddenly
turn and open wide a breathtaking expanse of
sky and green slopes and blue ocean rising up
to meet the sky -- and a tearful joy would well
up in me and drown me in a rapturous sweetness I'd never before known.

There were places where the dense pine
and redwood forests formed a canopy over the
narrow twisting mountain roads, and the light
would stream in green sprays and twinkling
raindrops of beauty through the trees -- and
I'd stoop by the bubbling stream to sink my
cupped palm into the pebbly cold water and
drink. And again, that sensation of chill
that caused the hairs of my neck to rise, and
the sweet delerious bliss of dissolving into an
inner light!

I was just a poor hermit of the woods,
singing the name of God -- "Hari! Hari!
Hari!", as I walked along in my clumsy rags.
I was a sweet bearded monk of the forest and
the world was in my eyes the beauteously
glorious form of the Divine -- all about me,
the playful sport of God!

II. THE COMMON VISION

I had come into the mountains to realize God, to know Him as Ramakrishna and others had done. But I also had an insatiable hunger to know about those saints of the past who had succeeded in their attempt to know Him, and to know how they had lived and how they had spoken.

The University of California was only a few miles away, and the University library was very complete. So, nearly every morning, I'd pack some bread in my sack and set out for the University, where I'd read for the whole day, or bring home some books to study. Though I was already familiar with many philosophers -- both ancient and modern, I voraciously read or reread every major philosopher and every saint in the Religion & Philosophy section of the University library, from the Greeks and early Christian Fathers to the Hindu, Sikh, Moslem, Taoist and Buddhist saints and sages. I read of Catholic monastic disciplines and Christian Science; I poured over the classics of medieval Indian and Sufi literature; I burrowed into the remote past through the long-lost writings of the Dead Sea scrolls and the Gnostic apocryphal books; I re-examined Heraclitus, Epictetus, Philo and Plotinus; and discovered al-Ghazali, Vidyaranya, Chaitanya and Shankaracharya. It was a glorious time of wild excitement and uncontainable exhilaration.

The *Upanishads* were a revelation to me. These scriptures of the ancient Hindus were as old as the Jewish scriptures, but their conception of God was quite different from the jealous tyrant the Jews had invented. He was knowable

7

as the one all-inclusive Reality, the one Self
of the universe. I could not help feeling that
there had been a tacit conspiracy in the Western
world by the church, the state, and academia
to conceal from me the fact that God could be
"seen" and known. But, of course, the truth
of the matter is that I was simply not ready
to grasp these ideas until this moment, and
it was only now that I was able to comprehend
what the *Upanishads* had to tell:

> He is beyond time and space, and
> yet He is the God of infinite forms
> who dwells in our inmost thoughts,
> and who is seen by those who love Him. [1]

> He cannot be seen by the eye, and
> words cannot reveal Him. He cannot
> be reached by the senses, or by
> austerity or sacred actions. By the
> grace of wisdom and purity of mind,
> He can be seen indivisible in the
> silence of contemplation. [2]

> He is the Eternal among things
> that pass away, pure Consciousness
> of conscious beings, the One who
> fulfills the prayers of many. Only
> the wise who see Him in their souls
> attain the peace eternal. [3]

Reading through the collection of writings
known as the *Upanishads*, I had a sense of
recognition, a recollection, of truths I had
known before. "Of course, of course," I kept
repeating as I devoured the words of the sages.
Nothing in the Western cultural tradition came
close to the penetrating subtlety and clarity
of the writings of these ancient Indian seers
who had penned these immortal scriptures.
But the West *did* have its seers -- though

they do not appear as early or as abundantly as their Eastern counterparts. In the West, the experience of unity, "the vision of God," is only vaguely implied by the early Greek philosophers such as Heraclitus, Plato and Aristotle. The later Stoics and Philo of Alexandria in the 1st century A.D. also refer only vaguely to such an experience, without any real attempt to offer a convincing account. In fact, it is not until Plotinus (204-270 A.D) that an explicit and unequivocal account of "the vision of God" is offered in the West. Here is his description of the experience in an extensive passage from his *Enneads:*

> The soul naturally loves God and yearns to be one with Him, just as a noble daughter naturally loves her noble father. ... And suddenly, [she] is uplifted and sees, without ever knowing how; ... the Supreme has come to her, or rather has revealed Its presence. She has turned away from everything around her and has readied herself, having made herself as beautiful as possible and fashioned herself in likeness with the Divine by those preparations and adornments which come unsought to those who grow ready for the vision. And she has seen that divine presence suddenly manifesting within herself, for now there is nothing between herself and the Divine. There is now no longer a duality, but a two-in-one; for, so long as that presence continues, all distinction between them is dissolved. The longing of a lover to unite with his beloved is a longing for a mere imitation of that divine and perfect union.
> ... In this state of absorbed contemplation, there is no longer a relationship

between a subject and an object: the
vision itself is the one continuous
Being, so that seeing and seen are one
thing; the object and the act of vision
have become identical ...

    ... It is a knowing of the Self
restored to its original purity. No
doubt we should not speak of *seeing*;
but we cannot help speaking in terms of
duality, such as 'the seer' and 'the
seen', instead of asserting boldly that
it is the attainment of absolute unity.
In this *seeing*, we neither regard an
object nor perceive distinctions; for
there are not two. The man is altered,
no longer himself nor belonging to himself;
he is merged with the Supreme, sunken
into It, one with It. ... Duality exists
only in separation; by our holding
ourselves apart from It, the Supreme is
set outside of us. This is why the
vision cannot be described; we cannot
separate the Supreme from ourselves
to speak of It, for if we have seen
something separate and distinct, we
have fallen short of the Supreme
which can be known only as one with
ourself.

    ... [In this vision] there are not
two; beholder is one with the beheld ...
The man who has experienced this mingling
with the Supreme must -- if he but
recalls It -- carry the memory of
Divinity impressed upon his soul. He
is become the Unity, and nothing within
him or without can create any diversity.
Nor is there any movement now, or passion,
or outreaching desire, once this ascent
is attained. Reasoning is suspended
and all intellection as well, and even --

to dare the word -- the very *self* is gone.
Filled with God, he has in perfect stillness
attained isolation, aloneness.
    ... This is the life of the gods and
of the godlike and blessed among men, ...
the passing of the alone to the Alone. [4]

After Plotinus, perhaps the most lucid and
explicit description of the experience of unity
comes from the 13th century German mystic, the
Dominican Prior of Erfurt, Meister Eckhart
(1260-1327). Eckhart's Sermons and other
writings were 'condemned' by the Catholic
Church in 1329; nonetheless, his writings have
carried the torch of mystical experience over
the centuries by which the way of many later
mystics has been lighted. Speaking of his own
experience of unity, Meister Eckhart declares:

In this breaking-through [of con-
sciousness], I find that God and I are
both the same. Then I am what I was; I
neither wax nor wane, for I am the
motionless cause that is moving all things. [5]
    I am converted into Him in such a
way that He makes me one being with
Himself -- not a *similar* being. By
the living God, it is true that there
is no distinction. [6]
    The eye by which I see God is the
same as the eye by which God sees me.
My eye and God's eye are one and the
same -- one in seeing, one in knowing,
and one in loving. [7]
    Here, one cannot speak of the soul
anymore, for she has lost her nature
yonder in the oneness of divine essence.
There, she is no longer called soul, but
is called *immeasurable Being*. [8]
    I found in me all things forgotten,

my own self forgotten and awareness of
Thee, alone, O God ... I found myself
with Thee, being Thy being and speaking
the Word and breathing the spirit. [9]

Here and there, I found other seers
scattered along the shores of time, from legendary
eras to the present: early Greek philosophers,
sages from the Vedic period of India, Moslem
Sufis, Christians, Chinese Taoists and Buddhists;
each telling the experience of unity in terms
that reflect the time and tradition in which he
or she wrote. The women, in most cases, tended
to color their accounts with emotion and allegory,
but it was clear that the experience had occurred
in them, and obviously showed no sexual bias.
In fact, it appeared that all sorts of people had
experienced the vision of unity; not only those
who could express it in philosophical or poetical
terms, but also simple good-hearted people who
have left us no record of their experience.

Of those who wrote, who recorded for
posterity some of the insights gained in that
vision of truth, were many who said little or
nothing of the experience itself, but confined
themselves to presenting a systematic philosophy
based on that experience; others, like the
prophets of early Judaism, wrote or spoke as
'holy men', feeling that they were chosen to
be spokesmen for God. And some, like the
Buddha and the yogis, in an effort to stem a
tide of futile intellectual speculation, declined
to speak at all of the traditional notions of God,
soul, and the nature of reality, but stressed
instead the need to practice those disciplines
which would lead to the direct experience of
Truth, wherein all doubts and speculations
would be resolved.

Naturally, each of these great beings
spoke in his own language, his own restricted

terminology, and the consequence is that today
we regard each of these efforts to reveal the
nature of reality as disparate and unrelated
'philosophies' or 'religions'. But the experience
of reality is the same for all, of course; and in
all the declarations of the many prophets and
Messiahs one can hear the attempt to convey a
common knowledge based on that common vision.

It was thus-I passed my days in the forest,
devouring the writings of the sages and saints
of the world in whose company I found great
comfort and happiness. During the day I read,
and in the evenings I sat quietly, happily, in
the presence of God. The growing clarity of
my understanding seemed to open my heart to
His ever-present reality, and little by little,
I grew more aware of and filled by His Love.
My intellectual curiosity had been satisfied; and
now there remained only the simple directing of
all my attention, all my thought, to the God
whom I desired with all my heart.

The author, Spring, 1966

THE KNOWLEDGE OF THE SELF

My little cabin in the redwoods was cool in the summer, but damp in the winter, as I discovered that first winter in '66. The creek swelled to a cascading Colorado river in my backyard, and I had to catch water coming down the slopes in little waterfalls to get clear water for drinking or cooking. I sat close to the cast-iron cooking stove, with the little side door open so I could watch the dancing blue and gold flames sizzle the oak logs and turn them to glowing ash.

Day and night, the rain drizzled outside the window in a steady, grey, time-dissolving continuum. I sat dully in the canvas chair by the stove, calling inwardly, "Hari! Hari!" In the mornings, I'd prepare oatmeal and a bath by the stove; I'd pour hot water from a pitcher over my body onto the concrete floor, and then sweep it outside. The rain would stop sometimes during the day, and then I would go out and walk the once dusty logging roads through the woods and up through the meadows in the high ground. "Hari! Hari! Hari!" was my continual call.

The dark skies kept my energies subdued, and my mind indrawn. My days passed uneventfully. It was in the night that the embers of my heart began to glow keenly as I sat in the dark, watching the fire contained in the stove. A stillness -- sharp-edged and intense -- filled my cabin and I spoke very closely, very intimately, with the God who had drawn me there. And He would sometimes speak to me in the stillness of the night, while I wrote down

His words.

Hari became my only thought, my only love. And while the days and nights became endless stretches of greyness, wetness, my mind became brighter and brighter with an intense light that displayed every wandering thought that arose as a compelling drama in bold technicolor and panavision; and then I would pull my mind back with "Hari!" I was resolved to refuse all envisualizations, all mental wanderings, holding my mind in continual remembrance and longing for Hari alone.

In the nights, my wakefulness burned like a laser of intensely focused yearning, a penetrating, searching light-house of hope in the black interior of the cabin, as I witnessed the play of the flickering flames dying out in the stove's interior. On one such night, I lit a candle; a song was being written in my notebook, and I was understanding very clearly, very vividly, just what it was that I loved, what it was that I was pledging my life to:

> *Thou art Love, and I shall follow all*
> *Thy ways.*
> *I shall have no care, for Love cares*
> *only to love.*
> *I shall have no fear, for Love is*
> *fearless;*
> *Nor shall I frighten any, for Love*
> *comes sweetly and meek.*
> *I shall keep no violence within me,*
> *neither in thought nor in deed,*
> *For Love comes peacefully.*
> *I shall bear no shield or sword,*
> *for the defense of Love is love.*
> *I shall seek Thee in the eyes of men,*
> *for love seeks Thee always.*
> *I shall keep silence before Thine enemies,*
> *And lift to them Thy countenance,*
> *for all are powerless before Thee.*

I shall keep Thee in my heart with precious
care,
Lest Thy light be extinguished by the winds;
For without Thy light, I am in darkness.
I shall go free in the world with Thee --
Free of all bondage to anything but Thee --
For Thou art my God, the sole Father of
my being,
The sweet breath of Love that lives in
my heart;
And I shall follow Thee, and live with Thee,
And lean on Thee till the end of my days.

November 18, 1966

This was the night I was to experience God.
This was the night I learned who I am. All day
long the rain had been dripping outside my
cabin window. And now the silent night hovered
around me. I sat motionless, watching the
dying coals in the stove. "Hari!" my mind
called in the wakeful silence of my interior.
During the whole day, I had felt my piteous
plight so sorrowfully, so maddeningly; 'Dear
Lord, all I want is to die in you,' I cried
within myself. 'I have nothing, no desire, no
pleasure in this life -- but in you. Won't you
come and take this worthless scrap, this feeble
worm, back into yourself!'

'O Father,' I cried, 'listen to my prayer!
I am yours alone. Do come and take me into
your heart. I have no other goal, but you and
you alone.'

Then I became very quiet. I sat emptied,
but very awake, listening to God's silence. I
balanced gingerly, quakingly, on the still
clarity of nothingness. I became aware that I

was scarcely breathing. My breath was very shallow, nearly imperceptible -- close to the balance point, where it would become non-existent. And my eyes peered into the darkness with a wide-eyed intensity that amazed me. I knew my pupils must be very large. I felt on the brink of a meeting with absolute clearness of mind. I hovered there, waiting. And then, from somewhere in me, deeper than I knew even existed, a prayer came forth that, I sensed, must have been installed in my heart at the moment of my soul-birth in the mind of God: "Dear God, let me be one with Thee, not that I might glory in Thy love, but that I might speak out in Thy praise and to Thy glory for the benefit of all Thy children."

It was in that very moment that the veil fell away. Something in me changed. Suddenly, I *knew*; I experienced infinite Unity. And I thought, 'Of course; it's been me all the time! Who else could I possibly be!' I lit a candle, and by the light of the flickering flame, while seated at the table in my little cabin, I transmitted to paper what I was experiencing in eternity. Here is the 'Song' that was written during that experience (the commentaries which follow each verse were added later):

O my God, even this body is Thine own!

Suddenly I knew that this entity which I call my *body* was God's own, was not separate from God, but was part of the continuous ocean of Consciousness. No longer did I feel separate from that ocean.

Though I call to Thee and seek Thee amidst
chaos,
Even I who seemed an unclean pitcher amidst
Thy waters --
Even I am Thine own.

Heretofore, I had called to God in the chaos of a multitude of thoughts, a multitude of voices and motions of mind -- the very chaos of hell. And in my calling, I was as though standing apart from God; I felt myself to be an unclean pitcher immersed in the ocean of God, dividing the waters within from the water without. Though God was in me and God was without, there had still remained this vessel of 'me'. But now the idea of a separating 'ego' was gone. And I was aware that I -- I too -- am none else but that One, and belong to that One, besides whom there is nothing.

Does a wave cease to be of the ocean?

A wave is only a form that arises out of the ocean and is nothing but ocean. In the same way, my form was as a wave of pure Consciousness, of pure God. How had I imagined it to be something else?

Do the mountains and the gulfs cease to be of the earth?

Mountains and valleys in relation to the earth, like waves in relation to the ocean, seem to have an independent existence; yet they are only irregularities, diverse forms, of the earth itself.

Or does a pebble cease to be stone?

A pebble is, of course, nothing but stone -- just as I now realized in growing clarity that I was none else but the one 'stuff' of Existence.

How can I escape Thee?
Thou art even That which thinks of escape!

Thought too is a wave on the ocean
of God. The thought of separation -- can
that be anything but God? The very tiniest
motion of the mind is like the leaping of
the waves on the ocean of Consciousness,
and the fear of leaping clear of the ocean
is a vain one for the wave. That which
thinks of separation is that very Consciousness from which there can never be any
separation.

*Even now, I speak the word, "Thou",
and create duality.*

Here, now, as I write, as I think of
God and speak to Him as "Thou", I am
creating a duality between myself and God
where no duality exists in truth. It is
the creation of the mind; having habituated
itself to separation, the mind creates an
'I' and a 'Thou'; and thus experiences
duality.

I love, and create hatred.

Just as for every peak there's a
valley, so the thought of love that arises
in the mind has, as its valley, as its
opposite, hatred. The impulse of the one
creates the other, as the creation of a
north pole automatically creates a south
pole -- or as to go "ahead" is to create a
"behind."

I am in peace, and am fashioning chaos.

The very nature of God's creation is
dual; He alternates in His own cosmic
rhythm from dormant to dynamic. In the
same way, the mind stilled is like a spring
compressed, representing potential release.

Peace, therefore, is itself the mother of chaos.

Standing on the peak, I necessitate the
                                    depths.

Just as the peak of the wave necessitates the trough of the wave -- since you can't have one without the other --, wakefulness necessitates sleep, 'goodness' necessitates its opposite. Exultation in joy is paid for with despair.

But now, weeping and laughing are gone;
Night is become day.

Now I am experiencing the stillness where this alternation, this duality, of which creation is made, is no more. It is a clear awareness that all opposites are derived from the same ONE, and are therefore dissolved. Laughing and its opposite, weeping, are the peak and the trough which have become levelled in the stillness of the calmed ocean, the rippleless surface of the waters of Consciousness. Night and day have no meaning here. All is eternity.

Music and silence are heard as one.

Sound, silence -- both are contained in the eternal Consciousness which cannot be called silent, which cannot be called sound; It produces all sounds, yet, as their source, It is silence. Both are united in the One of which they both consist.

My ears are all the universe.

There is only me. Even the listening

is me.

All motion has ceased;
Everything continues.

The activity of the universe does not
exist for me, yet everything is still in
motion as before. It is only that *I* am
beyond both motion and non-motion. For
I am the Whole; all motion is contained in
me, yet I myself am unmoving.

Life and death no longer stand apart.

The life and death of individual beings
is less than a dream -- so swiftly generations
rise and fall, rise and fall! Whole eons of
creation pass like a dream in an instant;
where then are life and death? How do they
differ?

No I, no Thou;
No now, or then.

Neither this individual being, nor God
exist now. Nothing can be said to exist
here -- but *knowing*. No now or then, for
time pertains only to the dream and has no
meaning here beyond all manifestation.

Unless I move, there is no stillness.

Stillness, too, is but a part of duality,
bringing into existence 'motion'. Motion and
stillness, the ever-recurring change, are
the dream of duality! Stillness without motion
cannot be. Where I am, neither of these
exists.

Nothing to lament, nothing to vanquish,

Lament? In the pure sky of infinity,
who is there to lament? What is there to

doubt? Where there is no other, but only this one, what is there to stand in the way of infinity? What is there other than me?

Nothing to pride oneself on;
All is accomplished in an instant.

Pride belongs only to man, that tiny doll, that figment of imagination who, engrossed in the challenge of conflict with other men, prides himself on his petty accomplishments. Here, whole universes are created in an instant and destroyed. Where, then, is pride?

All may now be told without effort.

Here am I, with a view to the Eternal, and my hand writing in the world of creation, in the world of men. What a wonderful opportunity to tell all to eager humanity! Everything is known without the least effort. Let me tell it, let me share it, let me reveal it!

Where is there a question?

Where everything is very simply and apparently myself, what question could there be? Here, the possibility of a question cannot arise. Who could imagine a more humorous situation?

Where is the temple?

The body is called 'the temple of God'. But when all is seen and experienced as one Being, where is that which may be regarded as the receptacle, the temple?

Which the Imperishable? Which the abode?

Which may I call the imperishable God, the Eternal? And which may I call the vessel in which God exists and lives? Consciousness does not perish. The Energy of which this body consists does not perish. All is eternal; there is no differentiation here.

I am the pulse of the turtle;
I am the clanging bells of joy.

I am everywhere; I am life! I am the very heart-beat of even the lowliest of creatures. It is I who surge in the heart as joy, as surging joy like the ecstatic abandonment of clanging bells.

I bring the dust of blindness;
I am the fire of song.

I am the cause of man's ignorance of me, yet it is I who leap in his breast as the exultation of song.

I am in the clouds and in the gritty soil;
In pools of clear water my image is found.

I am that billowing beauty in the sky; I play in all these forms! And the gritty soil which produces the verdure of the earth -- I am that soil, that black dirt. I am every tiny pebble of grit, cool and moist. And when, as man, I lean over the water, I discover my image, and see myself shining in my own eyes.

I am the dust on the feet of the wretched,
The toothless beggars of every land.

I live in the dust that covers the

calloused feet of those thin, ragged holy
men who grin happily at you as you pass
them by.

I have given sweets that decay to those
*   who crave them;*
I have given my wealth unto the poor and
*   lonely.*

I give to all whatever they wish of
the world -- but the wealth of my peace,
my freedom, my joy, I give to those who
seek no other wealth, who seek no other
joy, but me.

My hands are open -- nothing is concealed.

I have displayed all my wealth;
according to his understanding, according
to his evolution, each chooses what he will
have in this life.

All things move together of one accord;
Assent is given throughout the universe
*   to every falling grain.*

All is one concerted whole; everything
works together, down to the tiniest detail,
in the unfoldment of this world.

The Sun stirs the waters of my heart,
And the vapor of my love flies to the
*   four corners of the world.*

Like a thousand-rayed sunburst of
joy, my love showers forth as the universe
of stars and planets and men. And then,
this day of manifestation gives way to the
night of dissolution ...

The Moon stills me, and the cold darkness
*   is my bed.*

And the universe withdraws into utter
darkness of stillness and rest.

I have but breathed, and everything is
                              rearranged
And set in order once again.

The expansion and contraction of this
entire universe is merely an out-breath
and an in-breath -- a mere sigh;

A million worlds begin and end in every
                              breath,

And, flung out into the endless reaches
of infinity, worlds upon worlds evolve,
enact their tumultuous dramas, and then
withdraw from the stage once more. This
cycle repeats itself again and again; the
universe explodes from a single mass,
expands as gas, and elements form.
Eventually they become living organisms,
which evolve into intelligent creatures,
culminating in man. And one by one they
learn the secret that puts an end to their
game. And again, the stars reach the
fullness of their course; again everything
is drawn back to its source, ...

And in this breathing, all things are
                              sustained.

After this, I collapsed in bed, exhausted
by the sheer strain of holding my mind on so
keen an edge. When I awoke, it was morning.
Immediately, I recalled the experience of the
night before, and arose. I went outside to the
sunlight, dazed and disoriented. I bent, and
took up a handful of gravel, letting it slip
slowly through my fingers. "I am in this?"
I asked dumbfoundedly.

I felt as though I had been thrust back
into a dream from which I had no power to
awaken. My only thought was to return to that
state I had known the night before. I rushed
up the twisted road and scrambled up the hill
to the cliff on top of the world, above the forest
and ocean, where I had often conversed with
God, and I sat there, out of breath, praying,
with tears running madly down my cheeks, for
Him to take me back to Himself. Before long,
a chill blanket of grey fog, which had risen up
from the ocean below, swept over me, engulfing
me in a misty cloud. And after a few moments,
I reluctantly went back, down the mountain.

*   *   *

TWO

The Appearance Of Duality

"There is something hidden and perfect
Which existed before heaven and earth;
Motionless and fathomless,
It stands alone and never changes.
It pervades everything and is illimitable;
It may be regarded as the Mother of the
                                    universe."

                        -- Lao Tzu, *Tao Te Ching*

IV.   THE WAVE AND THE OCEAN

After some time, I adjusted to the fact that
I would have to live out my life in this dream-
like world. And I became very happy that I
had attained what I had come to the forest to
attain. For four more winters I stayed, happy
in my little cabin, but never again finding my
way to that place of stillness where my greater
Self lives. It seemed that my time of meeting
with the Eternal had passed, and a time of
preparation for the sharing of my knowledge
was now pressing me forward, for it was to that
I now felt my heart urging me.

But I was to learn that the experience of
unity, shared by Jesus, the Buddha, Shankara,
Plotinus, Eckhart, and many, many others, is
not so easy to speak of; for to speak of it is to
assert the paradox that the One is both an
unchanging constant *and* the very substance
of all phenomenal forms that we perceive as
inconstant and changing. To those who have
never experienced that Unity, such declarations
about It must appear illogical and self-contra-
dictory. This apparent contradiction can be
resolved and understood, however, if we recall
the analogy of the wave and the ocean:

Imagine, for a moment, that there exists
a wave who one day hears another wave speaking
of "The Ocean, Lord of all the waves." And
so, being intrigued, our wave sets out in search
of this 'Ocean'. His search leads him to a wise
old wave who advises him, "Look within, for the
Ocean is within you." Then, one day, while
concentrating within himself, the wave awakens

31

to the awareness that he *is* the Ocean. The
Ocean, he realizes, is the one reality that is
manifesting as all the waves -- and yet, though
the waves form and dissolve, form and dissolve,
the Ocean as a whole remains the same, continually unchanged and unaffected. This is exactly
what the mystic experiences in his awakening
to the universal Self: he is one of the many
manifestations, but he is also the one Reality --
unchanging, eternal.

Shankaracharya, the great expounder of
the philosophy of unity, called this apparent
duality between the many and the One, a
"superimposition":

> Like ripples on the water, the
> worlds arise from, exist in and dissolve
> into the supreme Lord, who is the
> material cause and support of everything.
> The manifested world of plurality
> is superimposed upon the eternal, all-
> pervading Lord whose nature is Existence-
> Consciousness, just as bangles and
> bracelets are superimposed on gold. [1]

Another way of explaining the "superimposition" of the phenomenal world on God is
by analogy with the ordinary experience of the
superimposition of a thought or image upon
one's own consciousness. Notice, for a moment,
how a thought is superimposed upon the background of pure mental awareness: it has a
definite reality, albeit a temporary one, and
yet it does not mar or alter in any way that
background consciousness. The thought- form
or image and the background consciousness
exist simultaneously, with a definite distinction
between them. However, the thought is formed
not only *on* consciousness, but *of* consciousness
-- just as a wave is not only on, but of, the
ocean.

In a way very similar to this, the phenomenal world of forms is projected upon the
supreme Consciousness: the world and God are
separate and distinct -- but the world has no
independent existence; it is formed not only
on, but of, God. In the mystic's vision, one's
own body is recognized for what it really is:
a form whose substance is the universal
substance; and one's consciousness is recognized for what it really is: the only consciousness there is. And then one knows that he has
no other identity, nor ever had, but the one
who alone is.

Though this realization was conceptualized
in a rational form in the *Upanishads* of India
long before such concepts were formulated in
the West, there were undoubtedly some few in
the Western world, even in ancient times, who
had experienced this astounding revelation.
However, there was as yet no language for
speaking of it -- save the language of myth.
For how was one to convey such knowledge?
How was one to speak of a reality which is both
One and many, both God and the universe? How
could such a paradox be made acceptable to the
philosophers, the scholars with their clever
logic? How could it be possible to explain a God
who creates without creating, who sets a universe
within Himself in motion without ever moving
or changing, who appears to be two -- a God
and a universe -- and yet remains One?

It became apparent early on that what was
needed was the introduction of two terms, each
to designate one aspect of this dual-faceted
Being, yet which would in no way represent two
separate and distinct entities, but One -- a One
with two faces. There was a need for one term
to represent the absolute, unchanging Godhead,
and another term to signify the creative aspect
which manifests the universe.

V.   CHRISTIANITY

In the West, Heraclitus was the first to introduce such a sophisticated concept of duality-in-unity, attributing to *Zeus* the power of *Logos* ("reason" or "order") to signify the universal divine Will by which *Zeus*, the unmanifested, created and governed the motion of all things. This term, *Logos*, was then adopted by the early Stoics, who likewise meant by it the creative Will or Power of manifestation which flowed from the Divine, and which constituted the phenomenal universe.

This conceptualization became immensely popular and widely acknowledged as a brilliant means of solving the old paradox of an un-moving Creator. But not until Philo Judaeus, a contemporary of Jesus, did the philosophy of the *Logos* reach its ultimate expression. Philo, an Alexandrian Jew, attempting to reconcile Greek philosophy and Judaism, artfully blended the rationalism of the one with the religious devotionalism of the other, characterizing the *Logos* as "the first begotten of God." "The *Logos*," he explained, "was conceived in God's mind before all things and is that which manifests as all things."[2]

Philo was a wealthy, aristocratic statesman and scholar; Jesus was a poor rustic. Philo never heard of Jesus, and Jesus never read Philo. Nonetheless, their vision was essentially the same. In order to show this, let me digress for a moment to briefly portray in capsule form the life of Jesus:

Jesus was a Jew, born in the town of

34

Bethlehem in Judea, and raised to manhood in
the town of Nazareth in Galilee during the time
of the Roman occupation. As a child, he was
steeped in the ancient lore of the Jews, and
he showed an acute interest in philosophy and
religion from the time of his early youth.
Around the age of twenty-nine (when Saturn
returns to its natal position), Jesus met a
teacher called John the Baptist, who served to
initiate the process of his awakening to the
divinity within him. Jesus then spent some
time in solitude, praying to the God whom he
addressed as his 'Father'; and one night, as
he prayed, he was drawn into a deep contemplation wherein he experienced the realization that
he and the Father were one -- that the one
Consciousness of the universe was who he really
was. It was a profound and lasting revelation,
one that overwhelmed all previous notions of a
separate, individual identity.

Jesus continued in solitude for some time,
reflecting on this new knowledge, and searching
his thoughts for some indication of what he was
to do with it. Many possibilities presented
themselves, but he knew in his heart that he
had no choice but to spend his life glorifying
among men the One who had so graciously
revealed Himself. Such knowledge could not
be withheld; it had to be shared with everyone.
It was the knowledge that would release men
from their mistaken ideas of the world, of their
bewilderment and despair, and herald a New
Age of joy. It appeared that it was he, Jesus
of Nazareth, who was called upon to be the
'Savior' whom the ancient prophets of the Jews
had spoken of in their predictions. And so Jesus
returned to his friends to share his "good news",
to tell others of what had been revealed in him.

Jesus recognized in the Psalms of David a
lineage of fervent devotion to God, a lineage

to which he himself belonged; and he sought
only to attest to and reaffirm that eternal religion
of Love -- the inner purification of the heart
which alone leads to the clear vision of God.
This inner vision Jesus spoke of as an entrance
into "the kingdom of God." But the orthodox
rabbis and religious leaders, unaware of the
fact of mystical experience, did not believe that
God could be 'seen' or known; nor did they
believe that they themselves were manifestations
of God. Such ideas went beyond their compre-
hension, and so were labeled heretical. Therefore the religious leaders of the Jewish
community accused Jesus to his face of
portraying God contrary to the traditions of
Judaism, and he answered: "You say that He
is your God, yet you have not known Him; but
I have known Him." [3] And he attempted to
explain to them that the consciousness within
them, the self which knows itself as 'I AM,
is the eternal God, the everlasting Self of the
universe, and could be realized through fervent
devotion and contemplation.

But the council of elders and high priests
were convinced that to allow the teaching that
man is God in essence would undermine all
morality, and would incite the people to
excesses; and so they voted to condemn Jesus
as a heretic, and they plotted to turn him over
to the Roman authorities as a criminal. Thus,
when Jesus came to the city of Jerusalem during
the celebration of the Jewish holiday called
Passover, he was arrested, tried, and condemned
to death by the high priests. He was then
turned over to the Romans and cruelly executed
by them.

The tragedy of Jesus was that of a great
lover of God who had realized the highest
knowledge, yet who was not understood by his
own people, and was slain by them. But his

tragedy served to uplift the consciousness of
the world, for today he is remembered and
honored everywhere as an inspiration to alll men
who would know God by the path of love and
who would manifest His Love in their very lives.

Jesus never adopted the concept of the
Logos, nor did he ever write out a concisely
formulated metaphysics; but though he often
referred to the distinction between the absolute
Consciousness and the world of matter as a
duality of the Spirit and the flesh, or of 'the
Father' and 'the son', it is clear that he never
regarded this duality as absolute and irresolv-
able; rather, he saw the flesh as a manifestation
of the Spirit, the 'son' as a manifestation of the
'Father':

> If you knew who I am, you would also
> know the Father. Knowing me, you know
> Him; seeing me, you see Him. ... Do you
> not understand that I am in the Father
> and the Father is in me? ... It is the
> Father who dwells in me doing His own
> work. Understand me when I say that I
> am in the Father and the Father is in me. [4]

Although the concept of the *Logos* -- a
creative energy projected upon the universal
Consciousness and manifesting as universal form --
was never recorded as a part of Jesus' teaching,
it is clear that had he known of the term, he
would have acknowledged its validity. The
author of the Fourth Gospel of the New Testament,
who lived about a hundred years after Jesus,
and who is known to us only as John, *was* familiar
with the term, however, and was most likely well-
versed in the writings of Philo. He adopted the
concept of the *Logos* and began his recounting
of the life of Jesus with these famous words:

> In the beginning was the *Logos* (often
> translated as "Word"); the *Logos* was with
> God, and the *Logos* was God (both separate
> from and identical with God).
> ... All things were made by the *Logos;*
> without him nothing was made. It was by
> him that all things came into existence. [5]

John went on, however, to assert that "the
Logos became flesh" only in the person of Jesus,
thus limiting and distorting the original meaning
of the term. For originally the *Logos* represented the universal creative energy which
"became flesh" in the person of each and every
creature in the cosmos. Later, in the 2nd
century A.D., during the years of struggle to
formulate a viable set of doctrines for a dis-
organized Church, Clement of Alexandria, Justin
Martyr and other Christian apologists vehemently
defended the Johanine idea that the *Logos*
became flesh uniquely and exclusively in the
person of Jesus of Nazareth; and thereafter,
the *Logos* became popularly regarded as a
term synonymous with Jesus, "the only-
begotten son of God." Since that time, the
Logos has so often been associated with this
idea, that it has lost much of its original
meaning.

VI.   SUFISM

Islam, founded in the 7th century by Muhammed, is, like Christianity, a monotheistic religious tradition that, while being an interpretation of the teaching of one particular religious teacher, is based theologically on the more ancient Judaic scriptures. And, like Christianity, its official philosophy is dualistic; that is, it holds that God and His creation are forever separate and distinct. Nonetheless, as in Judaism and Christianity, there have been occasional mystics within Islam who have not only realized but proclaimed that God, the soul and the world of matter are ultimately one; and, as in Judaism and Christianity, they have always been regarded by the orthodox of their own tradition as blasphemers and heretics. Thus, it is the common shame of these three traditions that the greatest of their followers, the most blessed of their seers -- their Spinozas, their Eckharts, their al-Hallaj's -- are invariably maligned and persecuted as heretics.

Within Islam, those seers who represent the mystic strain are called 'Sufis'. And in the early centuries of Islam many of these Sufis confounded the orthodox by speaking boldly of the unity which they had experienced of the soul and God. Abū Yazid al-Bastami (d. 875 A.D.) cried out, "Praise be to me!" Mansur al-Hallaj (d. 922 A.D.) uttered the famous, *'an al-Haqq'*, "I am the Truth," and added, "I am He whom I love and He whom I love is I. We are two dwelling in one body. If thou seest me, thou seest Him, and if thou seest Him, thou seest us both." [6]

But there were no true mystics who formulated a clear and concise philosophy of unity
until the gifted Muhyid-din Ibn ul-Arabi, known
in the West simply as Ibn Arabi. Born in Spain
in 1165 A.D., Ibn Arabi was a contemporary of
Saint Francis of Assisi (1182-1224), and of two
of the greatest mystic-poets of the Sufi tradition: the Persian, Jalal-ud-din Rumi (d. 1273),
and the Turk, Farid-ud-din Attar (d. 1230).
Ibn Arabi held a view identical to all others
who have clearly 'seen' the unity; he maintained
that the One and the many, the universal
Consciousness and the phenomenal universe,
are simply two perspectives on the same one
Reality.

The terms Ibn Arabi employed to distinguish
these two perspectives, or aspects, of Reality
are *Haqq* and *Khalq*. When we experience the
One (in the transcendent state of consciousness),
we are experiencing *Haqq*; when we experience
the world of multiple phenomena (through our
individual senses), we are experiencing *Khalq*.
"But," says Ibn Arabi, "the *Haqq* of whom
transcencence is asserted is the same as the
Khalq of whom immanence is asserted, although
the one is distinguishable from the other." [7]
Thus, Ibn Arabi's vision and his doctrine,
like that of the other great mystics of all
religious traditions is one of 'Complementarity'.

For him, the world (*Khalq*) is simply the
appearance of God (*Haqq*). It is simply our
limited perspective as individual perceiving
entities that produces the appearance of
multiplicity. "Multiplicity," he says, "is
simply due to the existence of different points
of view, not to an actual division in the one
Essence." [8] And Unity simply means that,
"two or more things are *actually* identical but
conceptually distinguishable the one from the

other; so in one sense the one *is* the other, while in another sense it is not." [9] "If you regard Him through Him, then He regards Himself through Himself [which is the experience of unity]; but if you regard Him through yourself [i.e., at the phenomenal level, through the senses], then the unity vanishes." [10] Furthermore, "if you assert that only *Haqq* [the transcendent] is real, you limit God. And if you assert that only *Khalq* [the immanent] is real, you deny Him. But if you assert that both things are real, you follow the right course, and you are a leader and a master in gnosis." [11]

Here, Ibn Arabi describes how, when the mystical vision of unity dawns, it is seen that the One alone exists -- and that It *is* the many:

> When the mystery -- of realizing that the soul is one with the Divine is revealed to you, you will understand that you are no other than God. ... Then you will see all your actions to be His actions and all your attributes to be His attributes and your essence to be His essence.
>
> ... Thus, instead of his own essence, there is the essence of God and in place of his own qualities, there are the attributes of God. He who knows himself sees his whole existence to be the Divine existence, but does not experience that any change has taken place in his own nature [consisting] of qualities. For when you know yourself, your sense of a limited identity [your 'me-ness'] vanishes, and you know that you and God are one and the same. [12]
>
> ... There is no existence save His existence. ... This means that the existence of the beggar is His existence and the existence of the sick is His existence. Now, when this is admitted,

it is acknowledged that all existence
is His existence; and that the existence
of all created things, both accidents
and substances, is His existence; and
when the secret of one particle of the
atoms is clear, the secret of all
created things, both outward and inward,
is clear, and you do not see in this world
or the next, anything except God. [13]

Though Ibn Arabi was never appreciated or
accepted by the legalists of Islam in his own time
or later, still his writings survived and had
great influence upon the more daring of
medieval thinkers -- within Islam and Christianity
as well.

Another mystic of Islam who deserves
mention was a great-grandson of Akbar, the
great Mughal king of India, whose name was
Dārā Shikōh (1615-1659). Dārā Shikōh was
tried and executed as a heretic by the fanatic
Muslim king, Aurangzeb, for having realized
and proclaimed the great unity underlying all
existence, and for teaching that the scriptures
of India, the *Upanishads*, also taught the true
knowledge of God. In his book, *Risāla-yi-
Haqq-Numā*, he speaks of his vision of Truth
in terms familiar to all who have seen:

Here is the secret of unity; O friend,
                     understand it:
Nowhere exists anything but God.
All that you see or know other than Him,
Though separate in name, is truly one
                     in essence with God.

Like an ocean is the essence of the
                     supreme Self;
Like forms in water are all souls and
                     all objects.
The ocean heaving and stirring within,
Transforms itself into drops, waves and
                     bubbles.

So long as it does not realize its unity
                     with the ocean,
The drop remains a drop;
So long as he does not know himself to be
                     the Creator,
The created remains a created.

O you, in quest of God, you seek Him
                     everywhere;
But, truly, you yourself are God, and not
                     apart from Him!
Since you are already in the midst of the
                     boundless ocean,
Your quest is like that of a drop
                     searching for the ocean. [14]

VII.   VEDANTA

Let us now turn to India, and trace the beginnings of the duality-in-unity idea from one of the earliest scriptures of which we know: the time-worn *Vedas*.

No one knows just when they were written, but scholars place this collection of poetic hymns and mystic lore in the second millennia before Christ. The earliest of the *Vedas* (meaning "Wisdom") are from a time of the most primitive agrarian society, and reveal a simple tribal mentality which regards the awesome mysterious forces of the universe as temperamental gods. Later additions to the collection, however, reveal a developing sophistication, presaging the later development of the monistic philosophy of the *Upanishads*. It is in such later Vedic hymns that we find the seed of the Hindu version of duality-in-unity:

> There was neither existence nor non-
>   existence,
> Neither the air nor the ether;
> For what was there at that time to
>   contain or cover?
> Was there, perhaps, only a vast and
>   fathomless sea?
> There was neither death, then, nor
>   deathlessness;
> Neither day nor night;
> Only *That* rested within Itself --
>   and nothing else.
> At first, there was only darkness
>   within darkness;
> Unfathomable depths of chaos enwrapped

the One:
And then, the formless Void stirred --
And thus the universal Form was born. [15]

It is this "stirring" itself that is the Power
of God. It is the creative Energy of the One
whose waves of vibration (represented by the
sound, "OM") gives form to the phenomenal
universe. But the question, "How is it possible
to 'stir' and yet continue to be the formless
Void?" had not yet been asked. This question
was to become the greatest puzzlement of both
Eastern and Western philosophy and the perennial
source of theological debate: How can God be
the Creator of the universe and at the same time
retain His motionlessness, His transcendence,
His Absoluteness?
    Those who have experienced the trans-
cendent Absolute say that during the experience
it is realized that, "all motion has ceased;" and
yet at the same time, "everything continues."
This paradox was also expressed by the author
of the *Isha Upanishad:*

It moves. It moves not.
It is far, and It is near.
It is within all this,
And It is outside of all this. [16]

But how is it to be explained? How can
it be logically spoken of? Before long, two
separate terms came to be used in order to
distinguish that which moves from that which
does not, that which is God's Power of creation
from God Himself. The unchanging God was
often called, *Brahman;* sometimes, simply "the
Lord." And His mysterious creative Power was
called, *Maya.*
    The concept of *Maya* can be found clearly
formulated in the *Svetasvatara Upanishad:*

> There is ONE in whose hands is the
> net of Maya, who rules with his power,
> who rules all the worlds with his power. [17]
>
> With Maya, his wondrous power, he made
> all things, and by Maya the human soul
> is bound.
>
> know therefore that nature is Maya,
> but that God is the ruler of Maya; and
> that all beings in our universe are
> parts of his infinite splendor. [18]

By the time of the *Bhagavad Gita* and
the *Puranas* (circa 500 B.C.), this terminology
was traditional:

> The Lord, though without form and
> attributes, ... has projected this
> universe out of His divine Maya. Having
> brought forth this universe, He dwells
> within all beings and within all things.
> Yet He remains unaffected, for He is
> pure Consciousness. [19]

But it was not until Shankara, the great
acharya (teacher, guide) of Vedanta, that the
principle of *Maya* was clarified and amplified
into a definitive philosophical concept.
Shankaracharya is believed by some to
have lived in the 7th century A.D.; others say
it was in the 9th century. At Sringeri Math,
one of the great monasteries established by
Shankara, there are documents claiming that
Shankara was born on March 25, 44 B.C.
What everyone does agree to, however, is that
Shankara was, along with the Buddha and
Jesus, one of the most profound thinkers and
visionaries who ever lived, whose teachings
have continued over the centuries to shape
and refine our vision of reality.
Like Jesus, Shankara died in his early

thirties, but not before he organized a number
of monastic orders, and wrote a number of
works in which he set forth a comprehensive
philosophy of Unity -- including commentaries
on the *Upanishads,* the *Brahma Sutras,* and a
number of independent treatises, chief among
which is *Vivekachudamani*, "The Crest-Jewel
Of Discrimination." In this small book, written
as a dialogue between a Master and a disciple,
he expounds the philosophy of superimposition
based on his own mystical experience.

Having experienced, during meditation,
an expansion of his normal consciousness to the
degree that he became aware that he was truly
the one Existence, the one Being who is all this
universe, he realized that the Supreme Self is
unlimited, undivided, eternal and unchanging.
This totality of Being, this universal Consciousness, he realized, was what the sages of the
Upanishads called *Brahman*. But, returning
to the limited awareness of the individual soul,
to the world of multiplicity, division and change,
he saw that this world is really not different
from *Brahman*. It is simply a different perspective on the same one Reality. *Brahman* is really
pure Consciousness, but somehow -- by a magic
known only to Itself -- It manifests as all these
forms which we call the universe. It is really
Brahman, but we call It "the universe":

> Brahman is the reality -- the one
> Existence, absolutely independent of
> human thought or idea. Though the
> universe seems to be composed of
> diverse forms, it is Brahman alone.
> ... No matter what a deluded man
> may think he is perceiving, he is really
> seeing Brahman and nothing else but
> Brahman. He sees mother-of-pearl
> and imagines that it is silver.
> He sees Brahman and imagines

that it is the universe. But
this universe, which is superimposed
upon Brahman, is nothing but a name. [20]

For Shankara, there is no real duality at
all between the Absolute *Brahman* and the
world, for the world is not other than *Brahman;*
it is an *appearance* projected, or superimposed,
upon *Brahman*, as we might superimpose the
mirage of a lake on a stretch of desert sand, or
as we might superimpose an imaginary snake upon
a piece of rope lying in the road. According to
him, the mystical vision reveals that there is
but one Existence; the world is not separate from
It, but is simply an appearance of multiplicity
of form where in fact there is only the one Self
of pure Consciousness. Nowadays, we would say
that *Brahman* and the world are 'Complementary'
perspectives on one reality, each excluding the
other, but both required to constitute and define the whole.
    This projection, says Shankara, of the
universe of forms upon *Brahman* is accomplished
by His own Power which is called, *Maya.* "*Maya*,"
he said, "is the power of the Lord. She is
without beginning, ... and is the underlying
Cause of all effects. ... It is She who brings
forth this entire universe." [21] *Maya* is not only
the supreme Power that generates and animates
the universe, but She is, at the same time, that
very universe which we perceive. She is at
once the Cause (the creative Power) and the
effect (the phenomenal universe). But, Shankara
reminds us, *Maya* is only an appearance; the
Reality underlying it is *Brahman*, and that is who
we really are. All the forms in this world,
including man, are the appearances of *Brahman;*
therefore, by understanding and contemplating
one's true Identity, says Shankaracharya, one
can free oneself from delusion, and experience

one's Self as *Brahman*.

Shankara's entire philosophy may be
summarized in one of his sayings:

> *brahma satyam*
> *jagat mithya*
> *jivo brahmaiva naparah*

> Brahman is the permanent reality,
> The world is an image;
> The soul of man, therefore, is nothing
> but Brahman.

Shankara teaches that, though our true
Identity is concealed from us by *Maya*, we can
dispel this ignorance through the practice of
discrimination, understanding that we are not
the body, the mind, or an individual soul, but
are, in fact, the uninvolved, eternal Witness
of the mind, body and the soul. By meditating
on this truth, he says, we can realize, and become
established in, the awareness of *Brahman*, the
Supreme Self:

> The Self is the ancient, supreme Being.
> It never ceases to experience infinite
> joy. It is always the same. It is
> consciousness itself.
> ... It is the knower of the activities
> of the mind and the individual soul. It
> is the witness of all the actions of the
> body, the sense-organs and the vital
> energy. It seems to be identified with
> all of these, ... but it does not act, nor
> is it subject to the slightest change.
> The Self is distinct from *Maya*, the primal
> cause, and from her effect, the universe.
> The nature of the Self is pure Consciousness.
> ... With a controlled mind and an intellect
> which is made pure and tranquil, realize
> the Self within you. Know the Self as the
> real *I*. Thus will you cross the shoreless

ocean of this world, whose waves are
birth and death, and live always
blessed, in the knowledge of identity
with Brahman. [22]

VIII.   SANKHYA

One can easily imagine the difficulties of explaining the principle of *Maya* satisfactorily, and of defending it against those who chose to ridicule it as a 'world-negating' concept. Perhaps for that reason, in another part of India, a different tradition had been formed along the same pattern, but employing different terms to represent the two aspects of reality. It was, in fact, one of the first efforts to put the expression of the duality-in-unity concept into an organized philosophical system, and it was attributed to an ancient sage by the name of Kapila. His representation of reality came to be known as *Sankhya* ("knowledge" or "wisdom").

Kapila asserted that there was an underlying universal consciousness that he called, *Purusha* ("Person") which was beyond all qualities and activities, and which was the true *Atman* ("Self") of all beings. And that the aspect of reality which was perceived as the multiform universe was an undifferentiated creative Energy which he called, *Prakriti* ("Nature"). Man's ultimate goal, according to Kapila, was to penetrate beneath the surface appearance of *Prakriti*, and realize his true identity as the one *Purusha*, the Self of all.

In Kapila's system, the creative Energy (*Prakriti*) itself came under thorough analysis for the first time. According to Kapila, this Energy consists of a binary polarization of force which, organized in an infinite set of combinations, produces all the forms of the universe. These polarized forces, or modes of Energy, he called, *gunas* ("strands"): one a

51

positive energy called, *rajas*, and the other a
negative mode called, *tamas*. Out of this
polarity, a third *guna* automatically comes into
existence by virtue of the balancing of *rajas*
and *tamas* when they are combined; for, when
a positive mode of energy is added to a negative
one, the result is a neutral mode of energy. This
neutral *guna* Kapila called, *sattva*. Together,
these three *gunas* constitute *Prakriti*; they are,
figuratively speaking, the 'strands' with which
She weaves this universe.

Thus, for Kapila, the universe of form
consists of one creative Energy self-divided
into a semblance of triplicity which, assuming
countless combinations, forms the atoms and
aggregates of atoms that make up the perceivable
world. How close this comes to what modern
physicists have theorized from experiments
several thousand years later, I leave for the
reader to judge.

In that great classic of mystical literature,
the *Bhagavad Gita*, written presumably around
the same time as the *Puranas*, Kapila's philosophy
found its fullest and most influential expression.
In it, Krishna, a manifestation of the Lord, explains to his disciple, Arjuna, the nature of
Purusha and *Prakriti*, and instructs him in the
means of transcending the *gunas* of *Prakriti*, in
order to realize his identity as the one *Purusha*,
the Supreme Self.

When a man's mind is under the predominat-
ing influence of *rajasic* (positive) energy,
Krishna explains, he is dynamic, excited and
assertive. When under the predominance of
tamasic (negative) energy, he becomes dull,
lethargic, and inert. When these two extremes
are purposefully balanced, they cancel each
other out, and a third and entirely new quality
predominates: a *sattvic* (neutral) energy by
which he feels calm, yet clear and awake. It is

this *sattvic*, balanced, mode of energy in which the mind becomes still, says Krishna, which allows for the possibility of seeing beyond the *gunas*, beyond *Prakriti* altogether, and thus experiencing the one *Purusha*, the primal source of all fluctuation and manifestation, the Self of the universe.

Philosophically, the system of Kapila and that of Shankaracharya are identical, and are differentiated from one another only by their terminology. For Kapila, the basic duality-in-unity consists of *Purusha* -- the eternal Self, and *Prakriti* -- the Energy which manifests as the universe of form; whereas, for Shankaracharya, these two same principles are called, *Brahman* and *Maya*. All other particulars, including the concept of the *gunas,* were identical in both systems.

Both of these philosophical systems, I would like to suggest, were born, not of a deliberate rational attempt to construct a plausible *weltanschaung,* but rather of an ineluctible vision, revealed to the mind in the transcendent 'experience of unity', though occurring to two different men at widely separated periods in history. It is a grave mistake, in my opinion, to view these two explanations of reality, as some historians and scholars tend to do, as mere intellectual constructions to be analyzed for academic categorization. They are both attempts, on the part of men who had clearly experienced the unitive Reality by the grace of God, to share their vision, their understanding, for the purpose of offering guidance to sincere aspirants to truth, and should be examined in that spirit.

IX.   BUDDHISM

In the 5th century before the Christian era, there lived in India a sage known as 'the Buddha', the enlightened one, who initiated yet another mystical tradition. Born into a princely life in the bustling town of Kapila-vastu (named for the sage, Kapila), in the kingdom of Koshala, young Siddhartha of the Gautama clan grew up amid wealth and comfort. He married and had a son. But at the age of twenty-nine, he suddenly struck out alone into the forest to enjoy the solitude and peace he felt necessary to the contemplation of truth.

Living alone in a wooded grove beside a river on the outskirts of a small village, Siddhartha gave himself to deep thought, en-deavoring to penetrate the mystery of existence. One evening, sitting beneath a sheltering tree, he experienced an un-precedented clarity of mind, and the unity of all life was directly revealed to him. Sudden-ly, his mind, free of its normal limitations, was the all-inclusive Consciousness of the universe, and all sentient and insentient beings were realized to be manifestations of himself. Never again would he imagine that he was just this one isolated self of Siddhartha; he was the Self of the whole world. Everything was now clear to him; and shortly thereafter he began teach-ing his message of Enlightenment to others and gathered about him a large following.

In those times, as now, men were of varying degrees of intelligence and learning, and therefore many different views on the

meaning and purpose of life were expounded.
The teachings of the *Upanishads* and the Sankhya
philosophy were known only to the few and
followed by yet fewer. For the most part, men
and women followed a less stringent regimen,
seeking merely to lead conventional lives of
piety and righteousness, giving respect to the
holy and alms to the poor. Incapable of sustained contemplation, they worshipped their
God through service and organized ritual.

The priests who directed the course of
these rituals were known as 'brahmins', as they
supposedly maintained an inner connection with
Brahman through the repetition of formalized
prayers from the *Vedas*, and through the ritual-
ized offerings of sacrifices, or *yajnas*. Thus,
the priesthood, supported by the populace,
maintained their positions as intermediaries
essential to religious worship by teaching a
dualistic philosophy based on the separation
between man and God (just as priests everywhere
have always done) -- a separation which could
be breached by their specialized intercession.

To the Buddha, however, such a religious
tradition was puerile and demeaning. He had
known the Truth directly, and he knew that
only this direct knowledge had the power to
satisfy the longing for certainty in every man,
and to free the mind from suffering and sorrow
connected with ignorance. And so, to the eager
and intelligent young men who flocked to hear
him, he taught the way of Enlightenment.

It is a fact of religious history that, when
the world forgets the true spiritual ideals, and
men lose sight of the meaning of life, 'reformers'
appear to lead men back to the fundamental and
ultimate goal of God-realization. The Buddha,
like all of the greatest of the renowned saints
of every land and every religious tradition --

Shankara, Rumi, Nanak, St. Francis -- was a
'reformer' in the sense that he served to recall
men to the perennial quest. He was a mystic,
one who had actually realized the truth of
existence, and who exhorted his brothers to
that same attainment.

The Buddha was not interested in mollifying
the weak; there were enough priests already
carrying on that work. Nor was he interested
in further involving aspirants to Truth in the
elaboration of metaphysical doctrines; his
purpose was to enable others to experience
what he had, for he understood clearly that no
ammount of indoctrination of metaphysics could
take the place of the direct and immediate
experience of Enlightenment, of *Nirvana*.
For this reason, he continually exhorted his
followers to the practice of self-introspection
and contemplation.

Despite the Buddha's refusal to elaborate
a complete metaphysics, a metaphysics evolved
within Buddhism, nonetheless, just as it must
so long as men think and speak. The one, the
ultimate Reality, which the Buddha experienced
came to be called, the *Dharmakaya* ("the totality
of Being"). Here, in a Buddhist scripture
called the *Avatamsaka Sutra*, the *Dharmakaya*
is described:

> The Dharmakaya, though manifesting
> Itself as the three worlds, is free from
> impurities and desires. ... It is forever
> serene and eternal. It is the One, devoid
> of all determinations. ... There is no place
> in the universe where It does not exist;
> but though the universe comes into being
> and passes away, the Dharmakaya remains
> forever. Though It is free from all
> opposites and contraries, still It works
> within all beings to lead them to Freedom. [23]

And, just as *Zeus* has its *Logos*, *Haqq* its *Khalq*, *Brahman* its *Maya*, and *Purusha* its *Prakriti*, *Dharmakaya* also has its inherent Power of Will which, according to the *Suvarna Prabha*, "creates all the physical bodies and subtle bodies, while the *Dharmakaya*, itself, does not suffer one whit of change on this account." [24] This Power of physical manifestation is called, the *Purvapranidhanabala* ("the primary power of Will").

So, as I hope the reader is beginning to perceive, the various "religions" and their attendant philosophies, differ from one another only in linguistic terminology. The experience they describe is one, and their intellectual conceptualizations of reality also are identical, despite the different terminologies adopted over the ages.

X.   SHAIVISM

India is a vast and ancient land, and her treasure of seers, sages and yogis is enormous. So it is not surprising that in yet another part of India, another tradition had been developing. It is perhaps the oldest tradition alive today, dating back to pre-Aryan civilization. It is known as *Shaivism*. In this ancient heritage, the aspect of reality which is Absolute and without attributes, the counterpart of *Purusha*, is *Shiva*. The creative-Energy aspect, corresponding to *Prakriti*, is *Shakti*. *Shiva* is a name used for "the Lord" since prerecorded time. Some of the oldest relics of mankind, found at Mohenjo-daro and Harappa, indicate that the great God, *Shiva*, was worshipped as far back as three or four thousand years before the Christian era.

Around the 8th century A.D., in Kashmir, a highly refined religious philosophy evolved which retained the old name, *Shiva*, as the name of the universal Godhead. It became known as *Kashmir Shaivism*. There are a number of philosophical works representing this movement, but its main text is a book of maxims of highly concentrated meaning said to be revealed by *Shiva* Himself, called the *Shiva Sutras*. With the intention of avoiding the difficulties of those who held that the universe was a product of *Maya*, the philosophers of this school made it very clear that the manifestation of the universe was not an illusion, but was as integral a part of God as light was of fire. They reiterated the old truth that the universe is an appearance of *Shiva*, a mani-

festation of *Shiva's* Power, or *Shakti*. The
term, *Shakti*, is of course synonymous with
Prakriti or *Maya*, but it was most carefully and
clearly defined so that there would be no mistake
that it was inseparable from *Shiva*, being merely
His 'Power of Will'. The *Pratyabijnahridayam*,
a medieval explanation of Shaivite tenets, leaves
no room for the possibility of an illusionist or
dualistic interpretation:

> The absolute Consciousness, of its
> own free Will, is the cause of the mani-
> festation of the universe. By the power
> of its own free Will, it unfolds the
> universe upon itself. [25]

In India, therefore -- as elsewhere in the
world --, we find an astonishing polyglot of
traditions intermingling and confused with one
another. But it can be seen that underneath
the apparent diversity is a very simple and
unvarying unanimity; as it is said in the *Rig
Veda*, "God is one; sages call Him by various
names." And His Power of manifestation --
whether we call it *Logos*, *Khalq*, *Prakriti*, *Maya*,
Purvapranidhanabala or *Shakti* -- is also one.
The vision of the seer has never changed,
though it has been told and retold in a million
ways, and in countless tongues, since the
beginning of time.

Over the centuries, India has seen the
development of countless expressions of the
mystic vision of reality; and always we find
this recurring pair: the Absolute and the
relative, the One and the manifold universe.
And invariably -- in the folk-art and in the
poetry of the people, these two are portrayed
as an inseparable and complementary couple --
as male and female, as Beloved and lover.
Sometimes they are represented in the person
of Narayan (Vishnu) and Lakshmi; in another

place they may be characterized as Krishna and
Radha; in yet other men's eyes they are the
mighty Mahadev (Shiva) and his consort,
Parvati (Shakti). Poets and artists make their
stories and their figures to represent these
two philosophical abstractions and thus tell in
their own ways the tale of the mystic's vision.
Thus we see, for example, a statue of Shakti,
wild-faced and arms akimbo, dancing on the
prone figure of Shiva in a graphic depiction
of the relationship between the One who is the
unmoving Ground and Foundation of all and His
active power of universal manifestation and
destruction. In the verses of the medieval
poet-saint, Jnaneshvar, these two lovers are
portrayed as, "the only ones who dwell in this
home called the universe":

> The supreme Reality which is One
> appears to be two. Through Her, the
> absolute Void became the primal Person;
> and She derived Her existence from Her
> Lord. Shiva formed His beloved Himself;
> and without Her presence, no Person
> exists. ... Because of God, the
> Goddess exists, and without Her, He is
> not. They exist only because of each
> other. How sweet is their union!
> The whole world is too small to contain
> them, yet they live happily in the
> smallest particle.
> They regard each other as their own
> Self, and neither creates so much as a
> blade of grass without the other. Because
> of Her, He assumes the form of the uni-
> verse. Without Her, He is left naked.
> Although He is manifest, He cannot be
> seen. It is only by Her grace that He
> appears as universal form. When He
> embraces Her, it is His own bliss that
> Shiva enjoys. He is the Enjoyer of

everything, but there is no enjoyment
without Her. She is His form, but Her
beauty comes from Him. By their intermingling, they are together enjoying
this banquet. [26]

It is a mistake on the part of students of
Indian culture to infer from her works of art
that India worships primitive gods, just as
it would be a mistake on the part of a student
of medieval Western civilization to infer from
the Cistine Chapel paintings that men of that
time and place worshipped a white-bearded,
muscle-bound God who imparted his spirit to
men with a touch of his finger.

Artists and poets have no other media by
which to represent The Formless except form;
their portrayals of God must necessarily be
figurative. And so naturally we find a great
abundance of religious symbolism in a culture
so religiously inclined: we find figures of
three-headed gods (representing the three
powers of Creation, Sustenance, and the
Destruction of the universe); we find multi-
armed goddesses of Destruction (representing
the multi-faceted reciprocal forces of Nature);
and we find the often-misunderstood *lingam*
and the *yoni* (representative of God and His
creative Power). But let us understand that
the visual and poetic symbols of *Shiva* and His
inseparable Power are symbols only, and point
to an extra-sensual and undivided reality; they
are merely reminders, expressions of a profound
understanding of the nature of our own Reality.

XI. KNOWLEDGE

Now that the two terms, *Shiva* and *Shakti*, have been amply clarified, I intend to use these terms throughout the remainder of this book wherever needed to represent the two respective categories of Reality which they have represented for many centuries. Please do not imagine on that account, however, that I am propounding a foreign or sectarian philosophy; I propose, rather, to offer these two as universal terms. We must remember that it is impossible to communicate without using *some* agreed upon terms, and yet whatever terms one uses must be foreign to someone. Let us agree, then, to use these two words as universal terms in order to avoid the confusion and misunderstanding which arises from purely linguistic differences.

The metaphysic I am presenting does not go by the name of Vedanta, Buddhism, Sufism, or Christianity. It has no name; it is only some knowledge that I wish to share with you. For I have not only arrived at these conclusions by persuasion of reason, but have also confirmed them by experiment; and I am merely attempting to present in the most convincingly rational manner the knowledge which I, and many others besides me, have acquired.

Throughout history, men have used various words for "knowledge". But there are, in fact, two different *kinds* of knowledge: there is the direct knowledge of the Self, or *Shiva*, which is perceived internally, called *Gnosis;* and there is the knowledge of Nature, or *Shakti*, perceived externally, which we call *Science.* Each kind of knowledge has its own methodology -- and its own limitations. Either kind of knowledge alone without the balance of its counterpart is extremely lop-sided and liable to error. "Science without religion is lame," said Albert Einstein; "religion without science is blind."

For a long time now, the civilizations of the world have recognized only science as knowledge. No doubt this has occurred as a reaction to the horrors and excesses of blind faith without reason or perceptible evidence. And now, the horrors of a science founded on reason and perceptible evidence alone, crippled by a lack of the sense of Divinity, are all too apparent as well. Hoping to understand reality solely through empirical, scientific study, we have groped and stumbled along, blundering often in the wrong direction; and finally we have come to see by our long efforts that what those mystics whom we regarded as dreamy fools had been telling us from the beginning is in fact the case.

Science -- especially that branch known as 'physics' -- through its unprecedented development during the entire 20th century, has revealed by its own methods a reality which corroborates the long-held claims of the gnostics. Acknowledging this, the well-known astronomer and author, Robert Jastrow, states that,

> For the scientist who has lived by his faith in reason, the story ends like a bad dream. He has scaled the mountains of ignorance; he is about to conquer the highest peak; and, as he pulls himself over the final rock, he is greeted by a band of theologians who have been sitting there for centuries. [27]

*   *   *

THREE

The Physics Of Unity

"The basic elements of the Eastern world-view are also those of the world-view emerging from modern physics. ... Eastern thought -- and, more generally, mystical thought -- provides a consistent and relevant philosophical background to the theories of contemporary science; a conception of the world in which man's scientific discoveries can be in perfect harmony with his spiritual aims and religious beliefs."

-- Fritjof Capra,
The Tao Of Physics

The descriptions of the universe by modern physicists are sounding more and more like the perennial descriptions by mystics of their experience of the transcendent Unity, the ultimate Reality. The convergence of the new world-view of modern physicists with that of the Eastern mystics is a fact much discussed in many recent books such as *The Tao Of Physics* by Fritjof Capra, *The Dancing Wu Li Masters* by Gary Zukav, and *The Eye Of Shiva* by Amaury de Riencourt. As Messr. de Riencourt notes, "It is the startling similarity between the world-picture of today's physics and the world-vision of Eastern Metaphysics that is perhaps the most outstanding cultural phenomenon of our times." [1]

Let me, then, reiterate the 'Eastern Metaphysic' so we can compare it with the world-view of modern physicists. As we have already shown, the mystics of the East hold that the universe is a manifestation of an insubstantial creative Energy which, vibrating into form, creates the entire phenomenal universe. This Energy, or *Shakti*, has no independent existence of its own, but is merely a projection upon a static background of pure Consciousness, or *Shiva* -- just as the thought-energy that creates dream-images is a projection upon the consciousness of an individual mind. Thus, *Shiva* and *Shakti*, the transcendent Absolute and the Energy which manifests as the immanent world, are simply polar aspects of the same one supreme Being. The duality created by dividing *Shiva* from *Shakti* is therefore clearly an artificial one, for they constitute an indivisible

whole. Nonetheless, the recognition of duality
within the whole is useful, for it reveals the
mechanics of the subject-object and the mind-
body relationships, which otherwise would go
unexplained.

Shiva refers to the Consciousness which
underlies Existence, not only on the universal
level, but on the human level as well. It is
the supreme Intelligence of the universe, and
it is also the light of awareness in man. It is
this underlying consciousness which gives life
to the mind and body. The body itself -- including the brain, nervous system, and all
functions -- is the creation of *Shakti*; i.e.,
it is a manifestation, as the entire universe is,
of the infinitely creative Energy which *Shiva*
projects. Thus, an apparent duality is created
between Consciousness and matter which
manifests itself in man as the duality of mind
and body, of subject and object -- a duality
that is *apparent* only, because they are ultimately undivided, constituting an unbroken
Whole.

XIII.   THE SCIENTIFIC REVOLUTION

The 'Eastern Metaphysic' just described represents a vision increasingly shared by Western science. While physicists are not likely to adopt the terms, *Shiva* and *Shakti*. the discoveries of 20th century science, won with such dilligence and dedication to the empirical method, continue to gather inexorably toward an overall world-view which clearly reconstructs and reiterates the model propounded by the Hindu sages thousands of years ago. Let us see how the scientific community has come to view the world as an embodiment of *Shakti,* or Energy.

The concept of 'Energy' was much discussed even by the middle of the 19th century. By this time, heat, electricity, magnetism, light and motion were already recognized as forms of energy; and von Helmholtz had postulated the Law of the Conservation of Energy, which stated that although energy could be changed into various forms, it could never by destroyed. But not until 1905, when young Albert Einstein published his Special Theory of Relativity, was it established that matter itself is a form of energy ($E = mc^2$). From that moment on, a new era had begun in man's understanding of the world in which he lived and moved and had his being.

Einstein had cracked the secret code of the universe; he had revealed the essence of matter, by proving that matter and energy are not two distinct and separate entities, but rather two different forms or states of the same thing. This was immediately confirmed in the laboratory, and nowadays it is a commonplace; physicists

no longer speak of *mass* or *energy*, but rather
of *mass-energy*. The interchangeability of
these two terms is so taken for granted that the
mass of subatomic particles is routinely measured
in units of energy (electron volts).

But the simplicity of this answer -- that
the universe is made of energy -- was lost on
nearly everyone. It didn't really seem to
answer all the questions, because what many
really wanted to know was not, 'What is the
world made of?' but 'How does it work?' It is
only natural that a man, even after he is told
that the ocean is only water, still might feel
that he must know something about the tides
and the nature of the current, etc., in order
to sail upon that ocean with the feeling that he
really knows what it is. And so, since the
beginning of the 20th century, physicists have
worked to discover how this stuff called mass-
energy works, and they've discovered that it
works in very strange ways. When we examine
it closely, it appears to be constituted of very
small particles of various sizes and proclivities,
some of which gather together to create
visible forms, while some others go flying
around the universe alone and invisible at the
speed of light. One of the most peculiar
things about these particles, or *quanta*, however, is that they behave on occasion as though
they were waves.

For every experiment in which a microphysical entity was proven to behave as a
particle, there was another experimental proof
that it behaved as a wave. The proofs mounted
on either side, along with the perplexity of the
scientific community, until at last, in the mid-
1920's, the Danish physicist, Neils Bohr,
realized what was right before everyone's eyes:
namely, that the wave and the particle are
really not distinct, but rather alternate,

partial images of the same thing. The microphysical entity we call an electron, for example,
can appear as a wave in a field of energy or as
a distinct particle, depending on the type of
experiment one sets up to measure it. In fact,
it is just the choosing of the type of experiment
to be used that determines whether one catches
a wave or a particle. This principle of duality-
in-unity Bohr called, 'The Principle of Complementarity.'

Einstein had earlier shown that mass and
energy are complementary images of the same
thing, that space and time are complementary
images of the same thing, and had hinted that
light-particles and light-waves are complementary images of the same thing, and finally Bohr
had declared that the two forms in which matter
appeared -- as particle and wave -- are likewise
complementary images of the same thing. Here
is how physicist Louis de Broglie explained
Bohr's idea of 'Complementarity':

> The entity "electron", as well as the
> other elementary entities of physics, thus
> has two irreconcilable aspects, which
> however must be invoked in turn in order
> to explain all of its properties. They
> are like the two faces of an object that
> never can be seen at the same time but
> which must be visualized in turn, however,
> in order to describe the object completely. [2]

Now, how is it possible to describe something that presents two mutually exclusive faces?
It is not even possible to say exactly where this
anomaly *is* at any particular moment. Is it a
point or is it spread out as a wave? Either way
one defines it, one excludes its complementary
aspect, the existence of which cannot be ignored.
So what is to be done?

The answer to this quandary

was an ingenious scheme devised by mathematician Erwin Schrodinger and others whereby an electron was represented mathematically as a probability existing somewhere within the defined space of a mathematical wave of possibility. Utilizing this device -- called a 'probability wave function' -- physicists are now able to predict the behavior of subatomic entities with great success, relying on the laws of statistical probability. Continuing with great dedication, they have probed more and more deeply into the behavior of matter, with the result of discovering more and more new kinds of wave/particles. However, as we shall later see, the cost of this ability to predict subatomic behavior was the replacement in the scientific lexicon of "real" objects such as electrons with mere abstractions; i.e., mere probabilities. But let us return to our immediate tale:

In the late 19th century, matter had been found to be divisible into molecules; then, molecules were found to be made of still smaller particles, called atoms; now, the atoms have been found to be constituted of yet smaller particles, such as protons and electrons, which fall into broad categories of hadrons and leptons. Some of these in turn appear to be composed of a yet tinier entity called quarks, which come in various "flavors". And so -- as of 1982 -- the fundamental constituency of matter, the elementary particles of which everything and every force in the universe appears to be made, is said by the physicists to be reduced to sixteen:

> 6 "flavors" of quarks:
>> up, down, strange, charm, top, and bottom.

> 6 kinds of leptons:
>> electrons, muons, electron-

> neutrinos, muon neutrinos,
> tauons, and tau neutrinos.

4 types of gluons:
> gravitrons, weak gluons,
> colored gluons and photons. [3]

But what are all *these* things made of?
Physicists, attempting to answer this question,
and to explain the apparently spontaneous
creation of all these so-called "elementary
particles," have theorized that these particles
have no real substance at all, but are mere
concentrations of energy arising from the inter-
action of invisible energy-fields. According to
this theory, called the Quantum Field Theory,
the *Field* is seen as the fundamental reality of
all phenomena, and the particles are merely local
condensations arising and dissipating within the
field. As Albert Einstein noted,

> There is no place in this new kind of
> physics both for the field and matter, for
> the field is the only reality. [4]

But Einstein himself was never satisfied with
the concept of a plurality of fields; from 1920 until
his death in 1955, he worked to formulate a mathematical proof of a single "unified field" that serves
as the source of all physical bodies and all interactions. Such a 'Unified Field Theory' would show
that gravitation, the weak, the electromagnetic,
and the strong nuclear interactions, are simply
varied convolutions in the fabric of the one all-
pervading space-time continuum. Recent advances
in technology and mathematical techniques are
now pointing the way to the completion of a
comprehensive unified field theory in the near
future. Noted physicist and author, Heinz Pagels,
writes in his book, *The Cosmic Code:*

Today theoretical physicists working
in quantum field theory have found
'grand unified field theories' unifying
the strong nuclear force and the electromagnetic and weak forces, and are
currently striving to incorporate the
force of gravity into this unification.
Should they accomplish this goal it
would be the completion of physics
as we know it now. [5]

Such a theory would signify the completion
of physics simply because it would answer all
the questions; all physical phenomena would
then become explicable according to the laws
of the one unified field. But what is this
"unified field" from which all of creation
supposedly proceeds? How are we to envisual-
ize it? We cannot; for it is again our old friend
with a new name: an all-pervading, intangible
and untraceable something, like nothing so much
as a universal Mind which projects thought-
forms upon its own screen. We may call it,
"a field", a "creative Void", or, borrowing a
term which has been used for over forty centuries to designate this universal source of
phenomena, we may call it, *Shiva*, and name
its power of manifesting as form, *Shakti*.

This concept of a unified field resolves the
age-old dispute of whether the world is made
of indivisible particles or of a single continuum.
The 'Field' is an invisible continuum which
appears as granular particles; i.e., as form.
The two apparently contradictory conceptualizations of reality are in fact complementary, each
representing the same reality from a different
focal point, or frame of reference.

From one viewpoint, the universe is immensely complex. From another viewpoint, it is
immensely simple. From the "simple" viewpoint,
the various forms that matter takes is not the

answer to what matter is made of; matter is simply made of 'the Field' (*Shiva*), in various degrees and permutations of vibratory excitation (*Shakti*), producing the illusion of form. These "illusions" may appear as variously flavored quarks, leptons, hadrons, nuclei, atoms, molecules or complete elephants; but no matter how intricately woven, the fabric of reality consists ultimately of a single continuum of potentiality which continually manifests and dissolves all these forms upon itself.

The investigations of physicists of the 20th century into the behavior of subatomic particles have led to revolutionary developments in all branches of science, medicine, and industry, enabling us to better understand the life-process and resulting in the saving of lives and in new means of power and communication. These scientists, with their cyclotrons and linear accelerators, have contributed immensely to the accumulation of knowledge of how the various elementary particles behave. But as to what these particles themselves are made of -- we already knew that: they're made of *Shakti*, the vibratory Energy of manifestation inherent in the universal Mind-continuum called *Shiva*.

XIV.   THE CONSTANCY OF THE WHOLE

Now that we have seen how the Supreme
Self is manifested in and as the phenomenal
universe, let us see how it is possible for the
Self to be, at the same time, the undivided and
constant Absolute:

I have already mentioned the Law of The
Conservation of Energy formulated in the mid-
19th century; let us now examine this Law --
also known as the First Law of Thermodynamics --
for it is this very Law of physics which explains
the existence of the absolute constant, the
unchanging Whole.

As originally formulated, the Law of The
Conservation of Energy stated that, "the sum
of the energy contained within a closed system
remains constant." What, then, is a closed
system? It is any operative energy system
which neither depends upon energy from, nor
transfers energy to, any system outside itself.
A closed system, in other words, is a 'perpetual
motion' machine in which the energy produced
is completely reutilized to power the system.
Imagine, for example, a gasoline engine so
enclosed that its energy-output was somehow
transformed back into fuel to keep it running
eternally without any loss of energy. That
would be a closed system. Obviously, such a
thing is not possible; there will always be some
loss of energy, through heat loss, etc., to
the surrounding environment. There is only
one *genuine* closed system in existence -- and
that is the all-inclusive universe, the Whole.
The Whole is the only closed system because

it is everything; there is nothing outside it to which energy could be lost.

An identical conservation Law was formulated to apply to mass, stating: "The sum of the *mass* within a closed system is constant;" but not until Einstein made it clear that the two terms, *mass* and *energy*, were interchangeable, were the two Laws combined into one to state: *The sum of the mass-energy within a closed system is constant.* It is this Law which makes possible the demonstration of the constancy of the Whole.

This Law, the Law of mass-energy conservation, asserts that, despite the incessant transformation of mass to energy, energy to mass, that occurs throughout the universe, THE SUM, the totality, remains constant, unchanged, undivided. In effect, this Law acknowledges an entity -- THE SUM, the Whole, as a distinct 'thing' over and above its constituent parts which possesses a quality that does not exist in its constituents, mass and energy: that quality is *constancy*. We see therefore that the Whole *is* something more than, and different from, the aggregate of its parts.

We may at first find it difficult to conceive of the universe as an unchanging constant, since there is seen to be so much change taking place within it. But, if we consider the universe as a *Whole*, then we must see that it does remain constant, since there is nothing in relation to which it can change. We may find it difficult at first to conceive of the universe as unmoving, since it contains so much movement within it. Still, since there is nothing else in relation to which the universe as a Whole can move, IT, the Whole, is unmoving.

The universe is the only thing that has this quality of *all-ness*, and therefore of constancy; and because there is nothing else like It to which It can be compared, we find it difficult to grasp with our minds just what It could be like. Nonetheless, the statement, "The Whole remains constant," expresses a very profound truth about the nature of the universe; a truth which is corroborated by the mystics. Jnaneshvar, the celebrated 13th century Indian mystic, speaks of It in the personal form, as *He:*

> Though gold may be wrought into many ornaments, its 'gold-ness' never changes. In the same way, He never changes, though the universe contains so many forms. [6]

In fact, *He* remains constant whether there's a universe or not. He (the Whole) remains constant when the universe is expanding; He remains constant when it is contracting; He remains constant when there is no universe at all. He is the same constant Whole even when the universal manifestation is only latent potentiality.

Let us make an analogy of the ocean. Imagine that the ocean is infinite: if we regard its 'water-ness', the ocean is one whole, and is constant. But if we regard its 'wave-ness', the ocean is multiformed and incessantly changing. Now, one may say that only the water is real because it is the constant substratum, and the waves are unreal because they are merely ephemeral forms. But another, who fails to make the generality, 'water,' and sees only the waves, may say that only the incessant motion of the waves is the reality, and the idea of a permanent underlying reality is only conjecture. A wise person, intervening, might point out to both parties that the ocean has a dual-sided nature. It is always the whole body of water, and is therefore a constant; and it is also the

moving forms of the water known as 'waves',
and is from that viewpoint changing and inconstant.

Similarly, from the standpoint of the One,
the universal Whole, nothing is happening; all
motion has ceased. IT is eternally constant;
It is *Shiva*. From the standpoint of the shifting
patterns of energy which make up the incessantly changing forms of matter, It is still in motion;
It is the inconstant *Shakti*. These two are not
even a hair's breadth apart; they are simply
two ways of looking at the same reality. They
are the same, but they are different.

This may be easily understood by a simple
experiment: Shut your eyes; become aware of
yourself as a single personal entity. You will
experience 'you' as a complete and undivided
being. Now, shift your awareness to your body;
become aware of the billions of cells being born,
living and dying within you in every fraction
of a moment. From this viewpoint, 'you' do not
now seem so single, so indivisible. Yet, there
are not two of 'you', but only one. It is similar
to the mystic's experience of the constancy of
the universe-as-a-whole, while simultaneously
experiencing the continuance of the motion within
the universe.

But how does this leap of consciousness
from the particular to the universal, from man
to God, occur? How does one become somehow
hooked to another 'wave-length' where he 'tunes-
in' on the Consciousness of the Whole? No one
can say, except to say, "by the grace of God."
What happens, though, is as mind-boggling for
a human being as it would be for a single cell
in my body if suddenly its consciousness were
to become 'switched' to my consciousness. "I
am not just this one cell!" we might imagine
such a cell exclaiming; "I am all these billions
of cells, and yet I am greater than the mere

sum of these cells -- I am this one being in whom
all these billions of cells exist, yet I am unaffected by their individual lives!"

We can scarcely conceive of how a single
cell in our body could be made to 'tap in' for a
time to the consciousness of the one in which it
lives and which, truly, constitutes its larger
identity, but this is much like what happens to
a human being by some mysterious process which
we call "grace", during the experience we refer
to as "union with God." No doubt, an individual
cell would speak of *its* experience in similarly
religious and mysterious terms.

One thing seems certain: when the experience of the Supreme Self is going to happen to
someone, that person's mind becomes automatically
withdrawn from concerns of a normal, practical
sort in regard to their individual life in the
world, and instead becomes centered on one all-
consuming love, a singular sort of love, for the
very source of love within. And in the process
of consummating this love, solitude is procured,
giving the mind the opportunity to become de-
tached from the pull of distracting thoughts
and sense-impressions, and the mind is then
focused with great intensity upon its aim.
Consciousness, like an unflickering flame in a
windless room, becomes pure and clear. And
then suddenly It knows who It has always been.

The experience of the Self, the unbroken
Whole, is preceded by meditation, prayer,
solitude -- but are these then the *cause* of
the experience? "No," say those who have
experienced it; "the cause is the unbroken
Whole itself. It is the cause of everything."

XV.   UNICAUSALITY

Let us look at *causes* for a moment. Most of what passes as scientific research is an enquiry into local causes. What causes cancer? What causes black holes? What causes poverty? And so on. Generally, we settle arbitrarily on a preceding event or state which we designate as 'the cause' of the present state. But scientists are realizing that the web of relationships is endless. They have begun to acknowledge that events are not caused by other isolated events, but are rather linked in a complex web of relationships within a larger common whole whose nature determines the nature of those constituent events. In other words, the primary reality is no longer thought to be the independent bits of which the whole is constituted, but rather the other way around: The primary reality is the Whole, the condition of which governs the functions and inter-relations of all constituent parts within the whole. The logical conclusion is that all local causes must be referred to the condition of the whole, which must in turn be regarded as the only actual *cause*.

Thus, in the new emerging wholistic world-view of modern science, the fundamental reality is *the unbroken Whole*. A remarkably lucid statement of this view which warrants appearing here in full is this from a 1975 article written by two respected theoretical physicists, David Bohm and Basil Hiley. According to them, the world which we perceive:

cannot properly be analyzed into
independently existent parts with
fixed and determinate dynamical
relationships between each of the
parts. Rather, the 'parts' are
seen to be in immediate connection,
in which their dynamical relationships depend, in an irreducible way,
on the state of *the whole system*
(and indeed on that of broader
systems in which they are contained,
extending ultimately and in principle
to the entire universe). Thus, one
is led to a new notion of *unbroken
wholeness* which denies the classical
idea of analyzability of the world
into separately and independently
existent parts. We have reversed
the usual classical notion that the
independent 'elementary parts' of
the world are the fundamental reality,
and that the various systems are
merely particular contingent forms
and arrangements of these parts.
Rather, we say that inseparable
quantum inter-connectedness of the
whole universe is the fundamental
reality, and that relatively independently behaving parts are merely
particular and contingent forms
within this whole. [7]

What this means is that local causes do not
exist in any real sense, since all relationships
are contingent on the condition of the whole,
and cannot be isolated from the context of the
whole.
Imagine a rolling wave on the ocean.
Does not each molecule of water in that wave move
in a place governed by, and interrelated with,
the placement and movement of every other

molecule? Are not each of the molecules of water forming that wave all moving "together of one accord?" Now, expand that illustration to include all the molecules of the universe. Are they not all rolling together interrelatedly and of one concerted accord? Is not the universe like one ocean, and the galaxies but eddies in that ocean? Where, then, in the midst of all this motion and expanse can one point to small-scale local causes between entities? Certainly there are countless interactions and relationships, but there is only one impetus, or cause, at the source of and governing all motion and all relationships.

If we must speak of *causes* at all, we must speak of the original Cause as the *only* cause, since the Initiator of the world-drama must be accounted responsible for all that followed the primary creative impulse. Imagine, for example, a number of balls on a billiard table. Each of the balls ricochets off the other in various directions, and one ball falls into the pocket. What caused the ball to go into the pocket? The last ball that hit it, of course. But what caused *that* ball to be rolling in that direction with just that ammount of force? Why, the ball that hit *it*. And what caused *that* ball ... etc. As you can see, by the process of regression of causes, we must eventually come to the initial strike of the cue ball by the cue stick. That, we say, was the primary cause of the ball's falling into a pocket.

Extending this regression of causes *ad infinitum* will bring us eventually to the one primary Cause from which all subsequent causes were produced, and in relation to which they all become effects. This 'Initiator' has been called *Shakti*, "the universal Will," "the unmoved Mover," and many more names. Whatever we call It, It is responsible for everything that occurs in this universe. It is the one Cause of all that has followed in an inconceivably complex chain of interrelationships. Not a single sparrow's fall, or tumbling of a grain of sand, occurs external to the universal order of unicausal progression.

While it is no doubt true that the world of sub-atomic wave/particles does not follow such clear-cut trajectories as billiard balls, and that the causal progression of their motions is entirely untraceable; nonetheless, the law of unicausality is never broken. There is, shall we say, an interlocking agreement, a perfect accord, in the working of the world, with no possibility of anything at all occurring out of order with the rest. And yet this order is not mechanical; it is more like the growth of a living entity.

Just as the growth of a tulip, filmed in time-lapse sequence, shows the beautiful, co-ordinated unfoldment of the whole plant to its glorious flowering, and subsequent demise, so does the unfolding universe display just such perfect organic coordination in its every detail. The point I wish to make is that in the unfolding of the universe, there are no small-scale *causes*; and yet there is an infallible causality at work -- as infallibly sure and definite in its working as in the unfolding of the tulip plant. For there is one primary Cause, and the universe following the unswerving laws of motion and causality, is its effect.

XVI.   THE PRINCIPLE OF INDETERMINACY

This idea -- of a universe of strict causality -- is in accordance with the world-view of Isaac Newton; but for many years now physicists have been questioning the validity of causality as a universally operative principle. It all began in 1927 with an article entitled, "On The Intuitive Content Of Kinematics and On The Mechanics Of Quanta," in which the Principle of Indeterminacy was first expounded by Werner Heisenberg.

Werner Heisenberg discovered the Principle of Indeterminacy (or Uncertainty) by a process of mathematics called "matrix mechanics" which, in effect, proved the practical impossibility of simultaneously determining both the position and momentum of an electron. The mathematical proof can be approximately demonstrated by the following illustration: Suppose you wished to illumine an electron with a photon of light in order to determine its position. You would find that each time you did, you drastically altered the position of the electron by that very photon of light. This is because to see something as small as an electron, one must use light of a very small wavelength, which is at the same time of a very high frequency; i.e., high energy. So, by pinpointing its position, you would inadvertently knock it helter-skelter, and hence lose certainty of its momentum. Conversely, if you used light of a longer wave-length; i.e., not so intense, you would get an idea of the momentum of the electron, but you would not have enough clarity to get an accurate 'fix' on its position. Or, if you tried another method, of narrowing the lens of the microscope, thus requiring less light, you would have a better idea of the path of the electron, but because light waves bend, or diffract, more as the aperture of the lens is narrowed, the distortion would cause the position to be obscured.

So -- what Heisenberg discovered was that, because of the very nature of matter and of light, the more clearly one was able to determine an electron's position, the more obscure became its momentum. And the more one focused on the momentum, the less information one could get about its exact position. In other words, no matter how carefully one attempted to measure the position and momentum of a particle, there would always be some uncertainty in the measurement. This is 'The Principle of Uncertainty'.

It became evident that one simply could not determine the causes of microphysical events; the ability to perceive the factors necessary to such a determination was precluded by the very nature of light and matter. For that reason, a group of physicists -- led by Neils Bohr -- renounced the attempt to describe the *exact* behavior of individual particles, and began studying the *probable* events in the sub-atomic world by means of statistical probabilities. By this method, they were not able to predict individual events, but could give the statistical probability for the occurrance of one possibility or another.

This was all very good, and very useful -- so far as it went. But then this group of physicists decided that since they could not observe and measure individual causal factors, then those individual causal factors *did not exist!* Bohr wrote:

It was necessary to give up describing the behavior of individual atoms in space and time according to the principle of causality and

to imagine that nature could make
amongst various possibilities a
free choice which was not governed
by any considerations other than
probability. [8]

According to this new brand of physics,
any given atomic particle behaves as it does
without any relationship to any event preceding
it in a causal chain: causality is not observed;
therefore, causality does not exist. This opinion,
held by Bohr and Heisenberg, came to be known
as the 'Copenhagen Interpretation' of quantum
mechanics, and was widely accepted by physicists
around the world as the only proper scientific
approach to quantum phenomena.

Unfortunately, this view cannot be contra-
dicted by empirical evidence, for it is no doubt
true that causal relationships on the subatomic
level are indeterminable by observation, as
explained by Heisenberg's Principle; but it is
just as undoubtedly true that such relationships
are not proven to be non-existent. To borrow
a phrase: 'Absense of evidence is not evidence
of absence.'

XVII.   BEYOND SCIENCE

Einstein -- along with but a few others -- protested the abandonment of causality. "God is sophisticated," he said; "but malicious He is not." Einstein argued that although quantum mechanics, utilizing the method of statistical probability, is successful in dealing with the problems of microphysics, it is not a *complete* theory, accounting for every element of reality, but is merely a stopgap measure to provide information in the absence of our ability to see the invisible progression of causes, or "hidden variables," which underlie apparently causeless microphysical phenomena.

Einstein continued to argue against the 'Copenhagen Interpretation' of quantum mechanics till the end of his life, often reasserting his belief that "God does not play with dice." Nonetheless, most physicists believed that even if these "hidden variables" or invisible causal progressions existed, they could never be demonstrated or calculated; therefore, it was pointless to regard them as relevant or meaningful to scientific endeavor. This position was very well summed by physicist Banesh Hoffman, in his book, *The Strange Story Of The Quanta:*

> As for the idea of strict causality, not only does science, after all these years, suddenly find it an unnecessary concept, it even demonstrates that according to the quantum theory strict causality is fundamentally and intrinsically undemonstrable. *Therefore, strict causality is no longer a legitimate*

scientific concept, and must be cast
out from the official domain of present-
day science. [9] (my italics.)

Let us follow very closely the logic implied
in the above statement:

(a) A legitimate scientific concept is one which
     is demonstrable by physical evidence;
(b) At the subatomic level, causality has been
     shown to be undemonstrable;
(c) Therefore, causality is not a legitimate
     scientific concept.

Here, we see clearly stated the inherent
limitations of empirical science, revealing its
inability to account for all aspects of experiential
reality. This is not intended as a criticism of
science; it is merely an acknowledgement of the
oft-recognized and understood principle that
science does not extend to the undemonstrable;
by its own definition, it excludes itself from
the realm of metaphysics; that is to say, the
postulation of undemonstrable causes. And
since Heisenberg has shown the impossibility of
determining or demonstrating the causes of subatomic events, then clearly, the postulation of
such causes cannot be a "legitimate scientific
concept" and must be cast out of its domain.
Nevertheless, we must see that it is equally
beyond the province of empirical science to imply,
as Bohr and his followers have done, that because
it is undemonstrable, causality at the microphysical
level *does not exist.* For, while it is certain that
science must dismiss causality from its concern,
that does not mean that causality does not exist,
or that it is beyond knowing. It is only by virtue
of the conceit that knowledge -- and truth itself --
is limited to the domain of 'science' that one can
uphold such nonsense.
Let us understand this issue clearly; it is

important to distinguish between *science* and *gnosis*, and to understand the capabilities and limitations of each: Empirical science is incapable of demonstrating causes; its only business is and has always been simply to describe the behavior patterns of phenomena. For though science is capable of describing the phenomena of motion, inertia, gravity, mass, space, energy, etc., it has never been able to determine the cause of these phenomena, as science is precluded in principle from the realm of the invisible, undemonstrable source of all phenomena, the *Cause* of the manifestation of phenomena. For the determination of the *Cause*, science must defer to the seers, the mystics. The role of science is then to show whether or not the statements of the seers are consistent with demonstrable evidence.

The knowledge of the mystics -- which we designate as *gnosis* -- is subjective and undemonstrable, but it is knowledge nonetheless. Gnosis is not simply a designation for any and every kind of subjective knowledge; it refers only to the form-transcending knowledge of universal Identity, the knowledge of the Absolute, the Godhead. Historically, this knowledge has been relegated to the category of 'religion', and equated with 'belief.' Yet it is, and should be re-established as, the summit of human knowledge, and the guiding light for science.

Science and gnosis do not contradict each other; they are complementary means of knowledge appropriate to a reality which consists of two contrary but complementary aspects. Gnosis looks to the realm of Consciousness, while science looks to the realm of phenomena; yet *both,* as complementary viewpoints, are absolutely necessary to the whole and complete knowledge of reality. Indeed,

it is the omission of either one of these complementary viewpoints that so often gives rise to
misunderstanding and error.

XVIII.   HELPLESS COGS?

As we have seen, Heisenberg's Principle shows, not that the world of matter does not follow the laws of causality, but rather that our ability to determine the subtleties of that process by empirical methods is precluded in principle by the nature of things. Isaac Newton's conception of a universe governed by its Creator and the laws of causality is not disproved, despite the many fervent attempts to make it appear so in various accounts of the "New Physics". But why, we may wonder, should anyone be fervently eager to disprove the notion of strict causality? Perhaps because it seems to threaten the sense of individual freedom. 'If the universe follows a strict law of causality,' some may reason, 'where then is my individual freedom of will?'

For some, the prospect of a universe of strict causality is a "dismal" one, which seems to reduce "the status of men to that of helpless cogs in a machine whose functioning had been preordained from the day of its creation." [10]   Yet most men of science find it necessary to acknowledge that if the universe *is* ruled by the principle of strict causality, then all men's acts, thoughts, desires are also governed by that principle. Max Planck, the founder of quantum mechanics, once said:

> The principle of causality must be held to extend even to the highest achievements of the human soul. We must admit that the mind of each one of our great geniuses -- Aristotle,

Kant, or Leonardo, Goethe or Beethoven,
Dante or Shakespeare -- even at the
moment of its highest flights of thought
or in the most profound inner workings
of his soul -- was subject to the causal
fiat and was an instrument in the hands
of an almighty law which governs the
world. [11]

We may feel, however, that we have some
freedom in our choices, that we are able to do
whatever we want. Yet we must recognize that
the "wants" which govern our "doing" are given
factors, results of previous causal factors. The
German philosopher, Arthur Schopenhauer,
noting this, remarked: "You can do whatever
you want, but you cannot *want* whatever you
want." Free-will is a chimera; it is simply
another name for an effect whose cause we
cannot see. This was clearly realized by
another great philosopher, Baruch Spinoza, who
observed:

There is in the mind no absolute or
free will, but the mind is determined in
willing this or that by a cause which is
determined in its turn by another cause,
and this by another, and so on to infinity. [12]
... Men think themselves free because
they are conscious of their volitions and
desires, but are ignorant of the causes by
which they are led to wish and desire. [13]

This may indeed appear a "dismal" view
to some, but really it is not so dismal if seen
in the proper perspective. In the context of
the unbroken Whole, men are not "cogs", but
instruments of divine Will, and expressions of
divine Joy. If the universe is to be seen as a
machine, it must be seen that it is a living one,
and that the life of the parts is the life of the

Whole. It is the Creator Himself who is playing
out the drama. Who, then, are the victims?
And who is the tyrant whose will is being
thrust upon us? *Us* is Him. And our willing
is His willing. Our dreaming and discovering,
our joys and despairs, and even our doubting,
is His doing. There are not two.

The universe *is* determined; it is determined
by the One who is manifesting as the universe.
But, though a man's life is destined, still he
is free. Man's true and eternal freedom lies in
his eternal Being; he may do only what lies in
his destiny to do, but he is always free in his
Being. He may be glorified or vilified, he may
be crowned or nailed to a cross; but as the One,
as the unchanging sky of pure Consciousness,
he is ever free, untouched by the raging storm
of the world.

Those who have glimpsed the unbroken
Whole and those who have not have always defined their positions on either side of this
particular issue. It is as old as man. Those
whose *I* is an individualized ego will always
protest: "Your determinism denies me freedom,
and therefore I cannot tolerate it!" And their
counterparts will always say: "I do not deny
your freedom. I only ask you to deny this
limitation you have placed on your identity.
See who you are! You are the universal Lord.
How could *your* freedom be denied?" But that
denial -- the denial of false self-identification,
or *ego* -- is a huge step to take, and is
taken only by those who have been graced
with understanding and true vision.

*   *   *

FOUR

The Psychology Of Unity

"Frequently consider the connection
of all things in the universe.
... Whatever may happen to thee, it was
prepared for thee from all eternity;
and the progression of causes was from
eternity spinning the thread of thy being."

-- Marcus Aurelius,
Commentaries

To the mystic, the one all-pervading Consciousness is the sole identity of everyone and everything in the universe; It is, without doubt, the ultimate Source and primary Reality from which the universe of form is projected. There is a movement among modern scientists, however, to view consciousness as a by-product of evolution, as simply an "effect" of the complex organization of matter. To the mystic, this view is absurd. It is like saying that a dreamer is the effect of a sufficiently complex dream, or that the thinker is the effect of a sufficiently complex thought. In order to clarify our understanding on this issue, let us examine for a moment the meaning of consciousness.

Consciousness is not easy for our minds to grasp, because we are it. It is closer than our jugular veins. It is the background of knowing, experiencing, being; it is the life that we regard as self. Consciousness can only be approached subjectively; what we know about it we know from introspection. From the standpoint of the Vedantic sages,

> The infinite, all-pervasive, all-supporting Brahman (universal Consciousness) manifests Himself as the *I* in man. He is the immutable witness of the functions of the intellect in this body.[1]

I am is an immediately evident fact -- perhaps the most evident of all facts. It is not necessary to think to be aware *I am* -- Descartes'

assertion to the contrary notwithstanding.
I am is self-evident and logically prior to
thought, for it is the *I* of *I think*. This *I am*
is synonymous with consciousness in man.
It is a constant underlying background which
serves as witness as well as substratum to all
possible mental states.

Just as the terms, *Shiva* and *Shakti*,
represent the apparent division of the One at
the cosmic level, the terms, *consciousness* and
matter (or 'mind' and 'body'), represent the
same duality on a human level. Consciousness
is the immutable, static witness; what it
witnesses is its own projection in the form of
thoughts, feelings, and images, as well as the
impressions registered by the senses. Consciousness is the seer, and everything else is
the seen.

Consciousness never vanishes; it is the
one unfailing constant witness to all the
various mental states: for example, in the
waking state, consciousness is the witness of
two simultaneous levels of activity; the
internal one of thoughts, imaginations, etc.,
and an external one of sense-data from the
'objective' world. In the *dream* state,
consciousness witnesses only on the internal
level, viewing the effusive activity of the
imagination known as dreams. And in the
deep-sleep state, consciousness finally gets
a break, as there is nothing at all to witness --
but itself. When waking from this state, we
say we were "unconscious", but actually,
consciousness was not absent; what was
absent was the thoughts, images, external
sense-data, and dreams. Consciousness
always remains; it is eternal. Even in deep-
sleep, though it is devoid of witnessing-content,
the *I* remains; otherwise, how would I recall
when I awoke that *I* slept soundly?

There is yet another mental state besides these three already mentioned; that is the state wherein consciousness transcends the Self-imposed limitation of a separate identity -- the illusion of being exclusively one particular body -- and recognizes itself as universal. The *I* experienced in this mental state is not a different *I* from the one which has always been experienced; it is the same *I*, but happily divested of the wrong notion of who *I* is. We may call this state, *nirvana, samadhi, satori, the mystic marriage, oneness with God,* or whatever we like; it is more precisely, however, the experience of the transformation of one's consciousness from its limited personal identification to an unimaginably pure and lucid awareness that: *I am the one Consciousness of the universe; all forms are my own!*

Returning now to the idea prevalent in scientific circles that consciousness is somehow the product of the organization of matter: perhaps now we can understand that what we see in the evolutionary process is not a production of consciousness from the sufficiently complex organization of matter, but an *emergence* of Consciousness from a Self-imposed state of involution, a state of lesser Self-awareness, to an increasingly greater awareness of Itself as the one Source and Substance of the entire universe.

As we have seen, in the previous chapter, matter *is* Consciousness in the form of wave/particles. Consciousness is the *only* reality. It manifests as the 'soul' of every sentient and insentient being, temporarily identifying with whatever form it takes; and, as the 'soul' evolves in understanding over the period of numerous lifetimes, Consciousness studies Itself in the mirror of thought, mental tangles become unraveled, and eventually the nature of the Self becomes evident to Itself. Consciousness thus plays a game of hide-and-seek with Itself, manifesting initially in ignorance of Itself, and through the process of soul-evolution, finally awakening to Self-awareness. In Its universal Totality (Its *Shiva*-aspect), It is always Self-aware; but in Its play as matter, life, and man (Its *Shakti*-aspect) It throws dust in Its own eyes for the sake of the game.

XX.   MIND

What then shall we say of the mind? If
we define *mind* in the simplest possible way as
the aggregate of thoughts experienced by an
individual, it is not likely that anyone would
deny that such a thing exists. Surely everyone
can verify the existence of thoughts. Then
the question arises, "What are thoughts?" And
the answer given by the yogis and Vedantic
philosophers is, "Thoughts are the vibrations
(*vrittis*) of consciousness." We should take
notice of the fact that thoughts, though register-
ing as electrical energy on the EEG machines
of psychological technicians, are formed of
consciousness. They must be understood as
both consciousness *and* energy -- in the same
way that a beam of light is understood to be
both a stream of particles and also a propagation
of waves. Thoughts also can only be described
from the standpoint of Neils Bohr's Law of
Complementarity, as here summarized by Werner
Heisenberg:

> The concept of complementarity is
> meant to describe a situation in which we
> can look at one and the same event through
> two different frames of reference. These
> two frames mutually exclude each other,
> but they also complement each other, and
> only the juxtaposition of these contradictory
> frames provides an exhaustive view of the
> appearance of the phenomena. [2]

It is obviously impossible to categorize
mind as either consciousness or energy; it is
both -- just as everything in this universe is

both. In fact, the manifestation of thoughts
(mind) by our own individual consciousness
is a process identical to the manifestation of the
phenomenal universe by the absolute Consciousness. In both cases, consciousness projects
a vibratory force which appears as form; it is
in this sense that man is said to be a reproduct-
ion of God -- made in His image. The difference,
of course, is that the private consciousness of
man produces a privately perceived world of
forms, whereas the universal Consciousness
produces a universally perceived world of forms.

Man and his mind is God's miraculous projection of Himself and His Shakti into the world
of His own creation. The attempt to analyze and
define the mind further is a fruitless endeavor;
it is more to our advantage simply to recognize
who we are, and to cease to identify with the
creative effusion of our minds.

It is the common experience of everyone
that thoughts continually arise on the surface
of consciousness. Day and night, the activity
of the mind is a reality that cannot be ignored.
Nonetheless, the underlying consciousness
remains as an unchanging background, an
imperturbable witness, to the continuing play
of thought. That pure sky of Consciousness
will always remain -- long after the body has
decayed, and the clouds of thought have
dissolved. That pure Consciousness is the
Self which you will always be -- unsullied,
unaffected by even millions of births, and
countless thoughts and dreams. Focusing one's
attention on that Self has the effect of
calming the stormy sea of thought, and
allowing the peace, clarity and joy of pure
awareness to be experienced.

In the *Pratyabijnahridayam,* a Shaivite
philosophical tract, it is said: "A man
becomes bound through being deluded by his

own Shakti." In other words, by identifying
with the contents of the mind, and forgetting
his permanent Identity, a man experiences himself as bound; and conversely, a man enjoys
freedom simply by knowing that he is the one
pure Consciousness, ever-free, ever-unaffected
by the tumultuous activity of the mind. For
this reason, the great Shankaracharya advised:

> One should understand the Self to
> be distinct from the body, sense-organs,
> mind, intellect and instincts, and always
> a witness of their functions -- like a king. [3]
> One should know, 'I am without
> attributes and actions, eternal, without
> doubts, unsullied, changeless, formless,
> ever-free and pure.' [4]
> The constant awareness, 'I am truly
> the Self' is the cure for the agitations
> caused by ignorance, just as medicine is
> the cure for disease. [5]

XXI.   SOUL

It is necessary now to say something about
the soul. The existence of thoughts, dreams,
images, and psychic impressions reveals to us
the existence of a reality that is subtler than
the physical reality experienced by the senses.
Shakti, or *Maya*, if you like, has created a
vaster spectrum of vibrations than just those
perceived by the senses. An examination of the
electromagnetic wave spectrum reveals a range
of forty-four octaves, from ultra-violet light
to long radio waves, of which only one octave
is visible light. The soul also is of a subtler
stuff than that we know as perceivable
"matter".

However, not everyone agrees on just what
the soul is. From the very remotest of ancient
times it was evident to man that the principle
of life was something separate from matter. For
as long as that mysterious factor animated a
body, it was alive and conscious; but when
life departed, the body became a mere lump of
decaying matter. Thus, it was apparent even
to primitive man that the world consists of two
separate principles: matter and spirit. Matter
could be seen and touched, but the spirit of
life was invisible and intangible; still, there
was no denying that the spirit really existed,
for it was obvious that a living body contained
a definite something that was absent in a
dead body; even a fool had to admit it. This
invisible spirit of life was called *pneuma*, or
psyche, by the Greek philosophers; to the
Romans, it was *anima*, or *soul*.

To the philosophers and theologians of

the West, this *soul* was conceived of as a
concrete individual entity which retained its
individualized existence for all eternity. But
in the East, the soul is regarded as identical
with the universal Self -- limited only by a
false sense of individuality, or *ego*. This
sense of individuality is regarded by Indian
philosophers as a mere ignorance (*avidya*) of
one's greater, universal Self. But this ignorance is not the ordinary kind of ignorance that
can be easily remedied by the learning of facts;
it is an ignorance that is 'God-given', and
which can only be dispelled by His Grace, His
Self-revelation. From this point of view, so
long as the illusion of individuality exists, the
soul exists; and only when this illusion is
dispelled by the inner revelation of the universal Self, does the illusion of a separate *soul*
cease to exist.

During the mystical experience of unity,
there is neither soul nor God, for that which
imagines itself to be an individual soul becomes
suddenly aware that it is the one and only
Consciousness of the universe. In that pure
Consciousness, there is no soul, no God; the
polarization of subject-object exists only while
the veil of ego-identification remains. This
is not to say that the soul is unreal, a mere
personal illusion, like a mirage; the soul is a
manifestation of *Shakti*, or divine Energy. If
it is an illusion, it is an illusion produced by
the supreme Consciousness; it is a product of
His *Maya*, and therefore as real as any other
of His manifestations. It continues its "illusory"
existence for lifetime after lifetime, and ceases
to exist only when He chooses to reveal Himself.

In every tradition of mystical philosophy --
whether Christian, Hindu, Sufi, or pagan
Greek -- we find complete agreement that the
personality, the individual consciousness, of

man is distinct from his physical body, and continues after the death of the physical body as a subtle form, or soul. There are differences among these traditions, however, as to how this soul comes to be and what happens to the soul after bodily death. According to those who believe the soul to be an eternally independent entity, there is a heavenly realm where souls dawdle away the hours singing praise to God for all eternity. According to the philosophy prevalent in the East, the soul continues to take birth in new bodies, evolving in understanding till at last it experiences its source, its universal Self; and then, after bodily death, continues to expand its awareness till it becomes entirely merged in and indistinguishable from the one divine Consciousness. This is the view expressed in the *Upanishads:*

> As rivers flowing into the ocean find their final peace and their name and form disappear, even so the wise become free from name and form and enter into the radiance of the Supreme Spirit. ... In truth, one who knows God becomes God. [6]

According to these ancient teachings, the soul does not reach its end in that perfect Purity, however, until it has rid itself of every impurity of ignorance, and is established in the awareness of the Self. And, as every soul must pass the same test of admittance to that realm of perfect Bliss, it is evident that, in the overall scheme, no possibility of injustice or favoritism exists. In a 'closed' evolutionary system such as this universe is, justice is complete and perfect; one cannot get out of it without going all the way to the end, and whatever wrong turnings are made along the way must be balanced exactly by corrections before the end can be reached.

To the ancient Greeks, this law of causality governing the subtle activity of the soul was known as the principle of *Adrasteia* (just retribution). It was supposed that, by virtue of this universal law, "we reap just what we sow." To the ancients of India, this principle was known as 'the law of *karma* ("actions")'. Implicit in this law is the reincarnation of souls as often as needed to satisfy unfulfilled desires, right wrongs committed in the past, and evolve toward perfection.

But why does God become individualized souls in the first place? And were they all made at once or at various times? I don't know for sure. And, judging by the variety of explanations available on the origin and destiny of souls, it would seem that no one really knows for sure how or why this process of individuation comes about. We can only surmise that it is God's sport or play. But I do know one thing for sure: that the dawning of enlightenment, the vision of ultimate unity, puts an end to individuation, and what we call the *soul*; for the final truth is that there is only one *I* who is playing all the parts of all the souls. And the realization of this is what is referred to in the scriptures as "liberation" from the wheel of rebirth:

> The realization of one's identity with Brahman is the cause of liberation from the bondage of rebirth, by means of which the wise man attains Brahman, the One without a second, absolute Bliss. It is this supreme Oneness which alone is real, since there is nothing else but the Self. Truly, there remains no other independent entity in the state of the realization of supreme Truth. [7]

XXII.   PERSONALITY

The soul in the above context is really
identical with personality. What I mean by the
word, *personality*, is the sum total of those
qualities that go to make up the uniqueness of
an individual, the stamp of individuality which
marks each being as a specific person. But why
this abundance of individual personalities? How
account for the amazing variety of personal
characteristics possessed by each soul? I would
like to offer an hypothesis:

Let us suppose that each personality/soul
corresponds to the planetary architecture existing in the heavens at the time of its terrestrial
birth, and is merely an expression of the universal energy-pattern existing at that moment
in space-time. Just as the destined role of
an atom is determined by the overall structure
or chemical organization of the whole organism
of which it is a part, is it not also possible
that each individual soul, or personality, fits
precisely into a larger overall scheme which
demands its appearance at precisely the time
and place, and under the precise circumstances,
established for it; so that it is sent forth into
the world on cue in perfect correspondence
with the planetary arrangement which defines
its being?

Throughout known history, men who have
studied the heavens have asserted that something like this was indeed the case, and that
a wise man could read the secrets of men's souls
in the movement of the stars. On this very
supposition, three Persian astrologers set out,
long ago, for Bethlehem, aware that whoever

was going to be born at that place at that time was undoubtedly a great being with a great destiny; for it was foretold in the extraordinary configurations of the planets scheduled to appear.

To discover such secrets, an astrologer draws a diagram of the positions of the planets at the time of an individual's birth which is, in effect, a still-frame in the history of the universe. It marks an exact and unique event in the unfolding of the universe of time and space which occurs only once. For that reason, it is an absolutely accurate indicator of the nature of life at that particular moment and place. The creature born at that juncture is, in a sense, an embodiment of the very unique arrangement of the stellar and plenetary bodies existing at that 'frame' in the unfoldment of the universe. The positions of the heavenly bodies are therefore related to the person born at a particular moment, not in any causal way, but simply by virtue of the fact that they are each embodiments of the same moment in the unfolding manifestation of the universe.

The discovery of Astrology -- the understanding of the relationship of planetary positions to the nature of each individual human soul and its destiny -- seems to have first occurred among the Chaldeans, a highly advanced people who, by 2800 B.C, had mapped out the constellations as we know them today, and had gathered centuries of scientific observations of the movements of the planets, enabling them to draw charts or 'horoscopes' ("to see the hour") for the birth of its citizens.

Babylon, following their influence, was said by Cicero to have spent four hundred and seventy years in collecting observations of the history of children born under particular combinations of heavenly bodies in order to perfect their astrological knowledge. This knowledge in turn was adopted and refined by the Persians, whose adepts

were known as *Magi*.   And throughout the West
this knowledge was disseminated by the Arabs
and Indian sages, resulting in its popularization
in medieval Europe. But with the decline of
philosophical learning and the rise of material-
ism and its technology in the West, Astrology
became, for a time, a lost art.

Today, however, there is a new
renaissance of mysticism in the West fostered
by the influence of Eastern thought, and it is
in this climate of renewed interest in the subtleties of natural philosophy that the ancient
principles of cosmic correspondence have re-
emerged into the light. In the next section,
we will examine these principles and take a
look at how they relate to the mystical
experience of unity.

CELESTIAL DYNAMICS
OF ENLIGHTENMENT

To discover the secrets of a soul's destiny, a map of the heavens is drawn for the exact moment and place of birth, which serves as a sort of 'blueprint' of that particular soul. But how, when, and in what sequence the events of the person's adventure on earth will take place is told in the *progressions* of the planets (one day in the ephemeris represents one year in the life), and by the daily *transits* (actual transitory positions) of the Sun, Moon and planets through the natal map.

All of the planets move through the twelve signs of the zodiac which comprise the 360° of the ecliptic; some slowly, some more rapidly. The Sun moves approximately one degree per day, and the Moon one degree approximately every two hours. The outer planets take weeks to move through a degree. But always the over-all architecture of this 'atom' which we call *the solar system* is altering its design moment by moment. And we, who are within the confines of this 'atom' are continually experiencing the changes in our own energy-patterns according to, and corresponding with, the changes in the angles from which the various planets and stars relate to us.

This implies, of course, that *everything* that happens to us in our lives will be accompanied by a planetary arrangement which, in its relationship to the positions of the planets at the moment of our birth, will symbolize that event. *If* this were true, we would expect, for example, that the unitive experience that occurred in me in 1966 would have been accompanied by

a singularly remarkable planetary pattern, a
once-in-a-lifetime lineup that unmistakably
corresponds to the nature of the experience,
involving planets and areas of the chart which
astrologers traditionally regard as of a
"spiritual" or "mystical" nature. Let us
investigate.

Here is a chart of the planetary arrangement in effect at the time of my 'experience
of unity'. In order to show the angular
relationships between these transitting planets,
I have drawn lines connecting those planets
in *opposition* (180°), *trine* (120°), and *sextile*
(60°) aspects to each other:

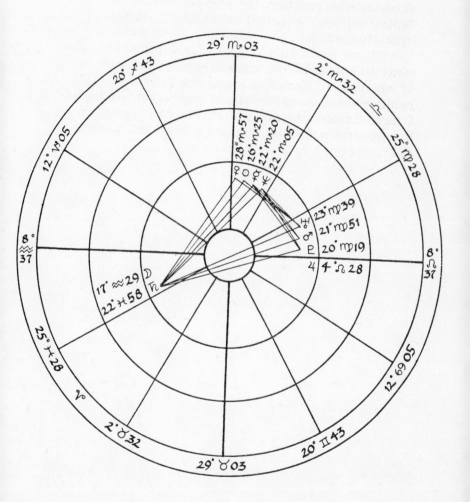

This, in itself, is a remarkable configuration. But now look at it as it is presented in relationship to the positions of the planets at my birth. Here is a composite chart, showing the positions of the planets in my *natal, progressed,* and *transitting* charts, shown in consecutive wheels. In the center wheel, my *natal* chart, calculated for 6:01 P.M., August 14, 1938, at Indianapolis, Indiana; in the intermediate wheel, my *progressed* chart for 9:00 P.M., November 18, 1966, at Santa Cruz, California; and in the outer wheel, the *transitting* chart for the same time and place:

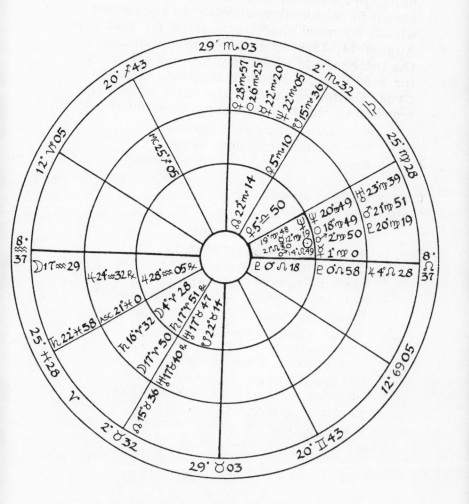

Natal Aspects:

    Sun conjunct Mars
    Sun trine Saturn
    Sun square Uranus
    Mercury trine Uranus
    Mercury conjunct Neptune
    Mars square Uranus
    Saturn semisextile Uranus
    Neptune trine Uranus

Progressed Aspects
(to natal planets):

    Sun conjunct Neptune (exact)
    Moon conjunct Saturn (exact)
    Moon semisextile Uranus (exact)

Transitting Aspects
(to natal planets):

    Sun conjunct Midheaven
    Moon sextile Saturn (exact)
    Moon square Uranus (exact)
    Mercury square Sun (exact)
    Mercury conjunct North Node (exact)
    Venus conjunct Midheaven (exact)
    Venus square Jupiter (exact)
    Mars conjunct Neptune
    Jupiter trine Moon (exact)
    Uranus conjunct Neptune
    Neptune conjunct North Node (exact)
    Neptune square Sun (exact)
    Pluto conjunct Neptune (exact)

(Note: planets within 1° aspect are considered to be exact.)

In examining this composite of charts, the first thing that stands out to the trained eye is the highly significant progression of both the Sun and the Moon (middle wheel) to exact conjunctions with natal planets (center wheel). The Moon's progression to an exact conjunction to my natal Saturn is a conjunction which occurs only once every twenty-eight to thirty years. The Sun's progression to the natal position of Neptune occurs in one's chart only if one's Sun position is natally within 60° or so, clockwise, of Neptune's position -- and then, only once in a lifetime. The likelihood of both the Sun and Moon forming progressed conjunctions to natal planets simultaneously is obviously very remote, and when it *does* occur, highly significant of an extraordinary event.

Neptune, to which the progressed Sun is conjoined, figures quite prominently in my natal chart, as it forms a conjunction to Mercury and a trine to Uranus. I had long ago come to look on it as a representation of a certain mental receptivity to poetic inspiration. But Neptune represents much more than that; with beneficial aspects from other planets it can represent an access to the very subtlest of spiritual realms. One astrologer, Robert Hand, who is a recognized authority on astrological symbols, says about Neptune:

> Neptune symbolizes the truth and divinity perceived by mystics. (Keep in mind that the planet is an agent or a representation of an energy, not the source of the energy.) At the highest level, Neptune represents Nirvana, where all individuality is merged into an infinite oneness of being and consciousness. [8]

Notice that the massive conjunction of transitting Mars/Uranus/Pluto (outer wheel) is

precisely over my natal Neptune, along with the
progressed Sun, and that the conjunction of
transitting Mercury/Neptune is precisely over
my natal North Node of the Moon. There were,
on that night of November 18, 1966, three exact
conjunctions of *progressed* planets to natal
planets, and ten exact aspects of *transitting*
planets to natal positions, five of which were
conjunctions. The concentration of energy over
my natal Neptune position was clearly intense --
intense enough for even a thick-headed person
like myself to catch a glimpse of God.

What does it all mean? Well, I think we
must say that, if indeed there is no real
correlation between the planets and the human
psyche, then what an extraordinarily grand
coincidence it is, what a marvellous accident
of nature, that at the same moment that I was
experiencing the Godhead, the planets were
proclaiming it in the heavens! I think we must
acknowledge that the significant planetary
picture at the time of my 'enlightenment
experience' does, in fact, seem to provide
evidence of the validity of that experience,
confirming that all things do indeed "move
together of one accord", that nothing happens
that is not ordained to happen, that the
universe is one co-ordinated Whole.

I would like to emphasize that the planets,
in themselves, do not have the power to
cause either good or ill-fortune, though
many habitually speak of 'planetary influences'
as though they were independent *causes*
determining our fate. In ancient times, of
course, as planetary configurations were seen
to correspond to definite kinds of psychological
and behavioral effects, the naive supposed
that planets were therefore independent

forces, responsible for the destiny of man. Each
planet was fitted out with its own individual
personality, and was assumed to have independent power to affect events on earth. This was
the basis for the myths of the 'gods'.

Plotinus, writing in the 3rd century A.D.
on the subject of *Are The Stars Causes?*, noted
that this belief is "tenable only by minds ignorant
of the nature of a Universe which has a ruling
Principle and a First Cause operative downward
through every member." [9]   He explained:

> Each [planetary] entity takes its
> origin from one Principle and, therefore,
> while executing its own function, works
> in with every other member of that All.
> ... And there is nothing undesigned,
> nothing of chance, in all the process:
> all is one scheme of differentiation,
> starting from the First Cause and
> working itself out in a continuous
> progression of effects. [1]

As the planets of the solar-system change
their angles to one another and thus rearrange
the structural design of the entire system,
there is a corresponding change in the energy-
pattern affecting the earth and its inhabitants.
Thus, the energy-pattern -- produced by the
angular positions of the Sun, Moon and planets --
which exists at the time of an individual's birth,
corresponds to the energy-pattern, or aggrega-
tion of qualities, of that individual soul. And
the subsequent alterations of the planetary
positions after that moment spell out in decipher-
able terms his or her destiny.

But -- and it is very important to understand this -- though the planets are instruments
by which the causal progression is transmitted,
they are not themselves responsible; they are

not the *cause*, but only the instrument of their
effects upon earthly life. In short, the
'influences' of the planets are really the
influences of the unbroken Whole, manifesting
locally as specific patterns of relationships.
The planets do not determine our fate; they
merely reveal it. Our lives are determined
by the One in whom the planets move.

The complexity of such a universe -- a
universe in which the destiny of each succeed-
ing soul on earth is in synchronization with the
ongoing motions of planetary bodies -- is indeed
beyond our ability to conceive. Nonetheless,
we must acknowledge that it is impossible to
separate the birth of any individual from the
cosmic conditions in which it occurs. For the
universe is an integral Whole, and every event
in it is in interlocking agreement with every
other; not even the tiniest, seemingly in-
significant, event may be considered as an
isolated phenomenon. Within this Whole, where
"all things move together of one accord," the
division of small-scale events into categories of
cause and *effect* is imaginary and has no real
meaning. For it is the Lord, Shiva, God --
call Him what you will -- who, by means of
His Power of Will, is the sole Cause of the
entire manifested array of the cosmos and
therefore of every single event which takes
place within it.

XXIV.   FREEDOM OR DETERMINISM?

The astrological correspondence to the experience of enlightenment leads us to some unavoidable conclusions: it appears evident that enlightenment, the vision of God -- whatever we call it -- is a fated and determined event. This is a staggering thought! "What, then," you may well ask, "becomes of the notion of Grace?" And I shall try to explain:

From our limited viewpoint in time, the experience of unity -- set as it is into the very pattern of the stars -- appears to be a thing of long-standing destiny. But *time*, from the viewpoint of eternal Being, is another thing altogether. To It, the entire universal cycle, from 'Big Bang' to final implosion, is but the blinking of an eye, the rising and falling of a breath. To us, it appears that such an experience is destined; but to the universal Consciousness, the revelation of Itself is an instantaneous and spontaneous act of freedom, and is therefore a matter of Grace, in the true sense of the word.

"But," you may object, "if every event in our lives is determined by God, where, then, is our freedom of choice? Where is the possibility for virtue, for choosing the path of righteousness over the path of evil? And how is it even possible to progress spiritually by one's own efforts if all is in God's hands? How can we be held responsible for our acts if every sentiment, emotion or thought is determined by God?

These are questions which must occur to anyone who thinks deeply about such matters. But these questions are framed on a presumption of duality where none in fact exists. *We* and *God*

are not two. And it is only a linguistic quandary
that we fall into when we regard ourselves and
God as separate entities, and consider one to be
determining the other. There is only One in this
universe; it is He who, as us, is freely making
all the choices.

Each individual being chooses according to
his or her evolutionary development, but it is
He alone who is manifesting as each individual
at every step on the evolutionary scale. Therefore, we must admit that everything is determined
by God's Will. And ... we must also see that,
since we are Him, we are free to choose. When
these two, *man* and *God*, are recognized to be
one, this question of whether we are free or
determined in our willing is easily resolved:
Determinism and free-will are *both* true; they
are 'complementary' truths, each representing
one aspect of a dual-sided reality. As the one
Consciousness (*Shiva*), we are forever free; as
individualized souls *(manifestations of Shakti)*,
we are determined by the law of causality, and
are therefore under the decree of fate.

Thus, the question, "Are we responsible
for our acts?" must be answered, "No," from
the standpoint of our individualized body,
mind, and soul; and, "Yes," from the standpoint
of the Self. For, as the one Consciousness, we
are the witness of all the thoughts and impulses
of our nature, and are free to grant or withhold
consent to her promptings. Therefore, ultimately, we *are* responsible for our acts. It is on
the basis of our Divinity that all civil and
criminal law recognizes the culpability of the
individual. For, if we were not God in essence,
if we were not absolutely free from causal
necessity, but merely unwitting, mechanical
pawns, we could not be held responsible for
what we do. But our Self *is* God, we *are* free;
and therefore, we *are* responsible.

The question of 'free-will' is one which has
facinated the minds of men since first man looked
to the heavens and deduced a Creator. And,
though the answer to the problem is very simple,
it is difficult for most minds to assimilate which
have not gotten into the habit of allowing for
two answers to be true which contradict each
other. Such an attitude is required of physicists
for whom light, and energy itself, must be seen
as both a particle (quanta) and a wave, whose
respective qualities are mutually exclusive. What
is required is the ability to freely shift one's
viewpoint from one frame of reference to another.

The answer to the question, "Do I have
free-will?" is determined by who *I* is. If you
are identifying with the body, mind and soul
(*Shakti*), the answer is, "No, you do not have
free-will." Nothing happens in this drama that
was not in the original script. Omar Khayyam
has rightly said:

The first morning of creation wrote
What the last dawn of reckoning shall read.

The Will that flung forth the universe is
its only Cause, and all that follows is effect.
All effects are implied and contained in their
cause, as the tree is contained in its seed.
Even your apparent choosing is *His* choosing;
even the choosing is Him. In short, there is
no escaping Him, for He is "even that which
thinks of escape."

On the other hand, if by *I* you refer to
the one Self, the universal Consciousness; if
by *I* you mean the eternal Lord and Witness of
all this drama, then you already know the answer:
"Yes, you have free-will. Your will is the only
will; You are Freedom itself!"

XXV.   THE PROBLEM OF EVIL

This brings us to consider why, if the one Self is making all the choices, does He so often make wrong, hurtful, and disastrous ones? Why, in short, is there *evil* in the world?

To answer this question, we must understand the evolutionary nature of *Shakti*. *Shakti,* God's power of manifestation, produces a drama which unfolds from a simple unity to a vast multiplicity -- from the first 'stirring' of Energy, to the formation of particles, to the structuring of chemical elements, to simple life-forms, to man, and ultimately to Self-realization. This is the process of soul-evolution.

Inherent in all of *Shakti's* effulgent production is the one Consciousness of which *Shakti* is the manifestation; It exists in and as every particle and force in the universe -- as the interstellar dust, as the rocks, as the plants, as the microbes, and so on. However, Self-awareness is merely latent, potential, until it has a fully developed human soul through which to function.

The ape is conscious; the dog is conscious; but not until the soul evolves to its fullest capability as man does Consciousness manifest Its full potential and become aware of Itself. All life is therefore an evolutionary game of knowledge-gathering toward the end of becoming fully developed and capable of grasping the answer to the puzzling question, "Who am I?" And this does not occur until man reaches his highest stage -- requiring a moral and intellectual development which can only be acquired over the period of many human lifetimes.

This leads us to answer the question about evil: In the process of evolution, while men are as yet unaware of their universal identity, mistakes occur, wrong choices are made -- just as children growing up make many mistakes before they reach adulthood. During this necessary process of evolution, mistakes based on an ignorance of the nature of reality can be extremely cruel and horrible -- evil, in fact. But although cruel and evil acts occur *during* the process of *Shakti's* unfolding, all evils and injustices are justly resolved in the completion of the evolutionary process.

On the subtle level of the soul, these resolutions occur by a reformation of the heart, or we might say, of the soul itself. There is no end to the soul's journeying until it has become "perfect as the Father is perfect." The same law of causality which is operative on the physical level is active on the soul level as well; we are able to reach the happiness of our true Self only by the perfection of our souls. It is in this sense that we reap just what we sow. For, just as the refinement of gold requires the burning of all impurities, likewise, the soul does not reach its final stage of Purity until it has passed through the fire of remorse which burns away all evil propensities, and until it has been proved worthy in the discerning eye of our own divine Self who witnesses all.

As it is said, "All's well that ends well;" and the consummation of the evolutionary process -- the knowledge and awareness of our true, universal Self -- reveals that the process of evolution is only a flimsy masquerade, that in fact we have always been free, always been divine and completely unaffected by the drama of *Shakti's* unfolding. It is true that evil exists in the process of evolution; but He who is projecting that drama is ever beyond good and evil, pain and pleasure; and that is who -- it must one day be realized -- we are.

   If we see truly, we must see that we cannot fail to reach eventually to our highest potential; for He, as us, will continue to choose according to the degree of our understanding. He will keep on striving, as us, to more thoroughly eliminate all error from our endeavors. It is His drama, and each act will unfold according to His script and His direction. It is He who is acting out all the parts, as us, and experiencing all the joys and sorrows as well as the transcendence of them. There is no advice to give, no correction to make; He is already in charge. He will continue to enliven our minds, to inspire our intellects, to illumine our souls. It is to ourselves that we must and will be true, for it is as our *Self* that He will lead us unerringly on our special way.

XXVI.   THE ULTIMATE UNITY

We live simultaneously in two frameworks
of reality; that of the divisible world of multiple
phenomena, and that of the eternal Self, the
unbroken Whole. All the great issues and
arguments of science, philosophy and theology
are solved in one stroke by the understanding
of the dual-sidedness of reality. From the standpoint of my *Shakti*-identity, my life in the
universal drama is fixed and determined. From
the standpoint of my *Shiva*-identity, as the
eternal witness, I am ever free. When I identify
as *Shiva*, I am the one all-pervading Soul of the
universe. When I identify as *Shakti*, the planetary configurations relating to my position on
earth strongly affect my mental, emotional and
physical being. When I identify as *Shiva*, I am
the Cause of all; I am the One in whom the
planets exist, and remain unaffected by the
changes taking place within the manifested world.
When I identify as *Shakti*, I am *Shiva's* servant;
I worship Him as my Lord. When I identify as
Shiva, there are not two, but only one -- and
I am He.

If we are to learn anything from this pro-
tracted examination of the dual-sidedness of our
own nature, it is that, if we can but peer beyond
the appearance of multiplicity, we can become
aware of the unity of all things, the unity and
ever-presence of God, the Supreme Self. With
such a refined vision, we will then be able to
see that not only are we the Self, but everything
around us is also the Self. The subject is the
Self; the object is the Self. Truly, no matter
who or what I see or speak to, it is really only

my own Self. If we could really grasp the truth of this, what a revolution would occur in our thinking and behavior!

Just as waves on the ocean are only water; just as golden ornaments are only gold, so all the various forms in the universe are forms of our own Self. Becoming aware of this, we would begin to revel in that joy which had been missing in our lives before. We would begin to drink the nectar of the unending Love for which we had been thirsting before. And we would begin to take delight in just being and living and acting in the world in a way we had been unable to before.

The knowledge once gained from an 'experience of enlightenment' is a means of escape from any real ensnarement in anxiety or fear from that time on. It is a background *knowing* which asserts itself when needed, and provides a surety which can never be shaken. The universal division into respective subjects and objects does not cease; the world goes on, even for the enlightened. It is just that he *knows* in his heart, with an indomitable certainty, that he and the universe are one.

Just as a chess-player retains the awareness that the antagonism between him and his opponent is merely a temporary game of role-playing, and that at the end of the game both the red and the black pieces will be thrown into the same box -- in the same way, one who has clearly experienced the unbroken Whole retains the knowledge of the ultimate Unity, and sees the play of subjects and objects as the ongoing pretense or play of the one Self.

Listen, again, to Jnaneshvar:

There is nothing else here but the Self.
Whether appearing as the *seen* or perceiving as the *seer*, nothing else exists

besides the Self. ... Just as water plays
with itself by assuming the forms of waves,
the Self, the ultimate reality, plays happily
with Himself. Though there are multitudes
of visible objects, and wave upon wave of
mental images, still they are not different
from their witness. You may break a lump
of raw sugar into a million pieces, still
there is nothing but sugar. Likewise,
the unity of the Self is not lost, even
though He fills the whole universe. He
is seeing only His own Self -- like one
who discovers various countries in
his imagination, and goes wandering
through them all with great enjoyment. [11]

*   *   *

FIVE

The Worship Of Unity

"Of all the means to liberation,
devotion is the highest. To seek
earnestly to know one's real nature --
this is said to be devotion."

> -- Shankaracharya,
> *Vivekachudamani*

"Devotion consists of supreme love
for God. It is nectar. On obtaining it,
man has achieved everything; he becomes
immortal; he is completely satisfied.
Having attained it, he desires nothing
else, he strives for nothing else.
Having realized that supreme Love,
a man becomes as if intoxicated; he
delights only in his own intrinsic bliss."

> -- Narada,
> *Bhakti Sutras*

XXVII.   DEVOTION

The two quotations which preface this chapter -- one by Shankaracharya, and the other by the legendary saint, Narada -- recommend precisely the same devotion to the very same Reality; but see how different are the words they use: one speaks of earnestly seeking "to know one' real nature," while the other extols the "love for God." Shankaracharya defines devotion (*bhakti*) as "continual meditation on one's own true Self." And Narada, recognized as the greatest ancient authority on the philosophy of Love, declares devotion to be "the constant flow of love towards the Lord." These two paths, of course, are not in any way different; meditation on the Self *is* the love of God. It is only that Shankaracharya identifies with *Shiva*, while Narada prefers to identify with *Shakti*. Both are methods of focusing upon the one Reality, and each, inevitably, produces the same result.

Nonetheless, this complementarity of identities necessitates two entirely different mental attitudes, or states of awareness: when we focus on the Self, we become aware: *I am the one infinite Existence-Consciousness-Bliss.* But when we take the attitude of love toward God, we become aware: *I am Thy creature and Thy servant, O Lord.* And it is the paradoxical fact that both attitudes are correct and valid which accounts for the confused oscillation many dedicated truth-seekers feel between the attitude of Self-knowledge (*jnan*) and devotion (*bhakti*).

I recall, for example, that, during the
time I spent in my Santa Cruz cabin, I had
a photo of the *jnani*, Ramana Maharshi, on one
wall, and a picture of the *bhakta*, Ramakrishna,
on the other wall. At one time, I would feel
entirely committed to the continued awareness
of my identity with infinite, unqualified Con
sciousness; at another time, I would feel certain
that devotional love for God was the only
attitude for me. Since both of these identities
co-exist in everyone, both of these mental
attitudes co-exist in everyone as well --
though one or the other is normally predominant,
depending upon one's temperament.

To say, "I am God," as Mansur al-Hallaj
did, is offensive to the *bhakta*, for it denies
the separate existence and fallibility of the
individual soul; and to say, "I am the servant
of God," does not satisfy the *jnani*, for it
asserts a duality where none in fact exists.
I am convinced that, if we are to speak truly
and to live realistically, it is necessary to embrace
both attitudes, and to relinquish the logic which
begs for an either/or approach to identity.
The greatest contemplatives who've ever lived,
having pondered this quandary, have come to
the same conclusion, and have taken a position
which defies categorization into one classification
or another. For example, the Blessed Jan
Ruysbroeck, a 14th century disciple of Meister
Eckhart, wrote:

> Though I have said before that we
> are one with God, ... yet now I will say
> that we must eternally remain other than
> God, and distinct from Him. ... And
> we must understand and feel *both*
> within us, if all is to be right with us. [1]

And in the following song of a famous 15th
century poet-saint of India, the incomparable

Kabir, we can hear the perfect blending of the
devotion of the *bhakta* and the unitive knowledge
of the *jnani:*

> O brothers, the Love of God is sweet!
> Wherever I go, I offer salutations to
>   the Lord;
> Whatever I do is an act of worship to Him.
> In sleep, I reverence Him; I bow my knee
>   to no other.
> Whatever I utter is His Name;
> Whatever I hear reminds me of Him.
> Whatever I eat or drink is to His honor.
> To me society and solitude are one,
> For all feelings of duality have left me.
> I have no need to practice austerity,
> For I see Him smiling everywhere
> As the supreme Beauty in every form.
> Whether sitting, walking or performing
>   actions,
> My heart remains pure, for my mind remains
>   fixed on God.
> Says Kabir: "I have exper enc d the
>   divi e state
> Beyond joy and suffering, and I am
>   absorbed in That."
> O brothers, the Love of God is sweet! [2]

Just as *Shiva* and *Shakti* cannot be separated
one from the other, neither can the *jnani* and
the *bhakta* be separated; though mutually exclusive, they co-exist as complements in everyone.
And as our knowledge grows, we must learn to
adapt our vision of the world to accept and
embrace apparently contradictory views. We
must learn to feel comfortable with the notion
that a quantity of energy is both a wave and
a quantum; that our lives are determined, *and*
that we are free; that our identity is both the
Whole *and* the part. We are the universal Self;
we *are* God -- and we are also the individualized

'soul' which consists of the mind and its own
private impressions. We are the Ocean -- but
we are also the wave.

    We are *Shiva,* but we are also *Shakti.*
We are perfect, but we are also imperfect.
We are the eternal Reality, but we are also
the ephemeral image It projects on Its own
screen. We are indeed the Dreamer, but we are
also the dream. We are entitled to say, "I am
Shiva," but so long as the *Shakti*-mind exists,
it must sing the song of Love and devotion to
its Lord. While we live and move in this
phantasmagoria, we are His creatures, and
are utterly dependent upon His grace. Therefore, if we truly understand our own double-
faceted reality, we must learn to sing two
songs: one, the song of our own immortal
Self; and the other, the song of Love.
Neither, without the other, is complete.

XXVIII.   GRACE

Just as there are many *bhaktas* who refuse
to acknowledge man's identity as God, there are
also many *jnanis* who refuse to open their hearts
to the Love of God, protesting that the fact of
Unity precludes such an attitude, and that the
preservation of an I-Thou relationship only
prolongs the delusion of duality. I would like
to point out to such people that so long as we
are not lifted into the experience of unity by
the Grace of God, duality continues to exist for
us -- whether we admit to it or not. The Grace
of God is an experience of Love, a Love that
draws us to the experience of unity. Without
it, we can never know the Self.

The Love of God is not a love between a
subject and an object; for in this case, the subject, the object, and the Love itself, are one.
Nor is this Love the result of a conclusion based
on a rational premise; it is an inner experience.
It is something quite real -- breathtakingly and
intoxicatingly real. It stirs from within, and
centers on itself within. It is not a thought-
out construction based on philosophical reasoning,
but a sweetness that is itself the object of
devotion. It is this Love that *bhaktas* love. It
has no location but the human heart, yet its
source is the universal Being. It is His gracious
gift, and only those who have experienced it
know what it is.

It is of this Love that Sri Ramakrishna sang:

How are you trying, O my mind, to know
                    the nature of God?
You are groping like a madman locked in

> a dark room.
> He is grasped through ecstatic love;
> How can you fathom Him without it?
> When that Love awakes, the Lord,
> Like a magnet, draws to Him the soul. [3]

Such longing for God always precedes the experience of enlightenment because it is the natural expression, the indicator, of a shift in the consciousness toward the transcendent Unity. All of the outer events as well as the inner ones will conspire to bring one's life to that point where enlightenment is experienced. When it is time for it to come, it will produce itself, and it will announce its coming by a great wave of Love that steers the heart irresistably to the source of that Love, and eventually reveals itself unaided from within.

Consider the great Shankaracharya's final message to the disciple in his *Viveka-chudamani*:

> Gurus and scriptures can
> stimulate spiritual awareness,
> but one crosses the ocean of
> ignorance only by direct illum-
> ination, *through the grace of God.* [4]

No one has ever realized God except those to whom He has revealed Himself. On this point all Self-realized beings are unanimously agreed. As one commentator says, in the *Malini Vijaya Vartika:* "The learned men of all times always hold that the descent of Grace does not have any cause or condition, but depends entirely on the free will of the Lord." If it were dependent upon conditions, it would not be absolute and independent 'Grace'. According to yet another Eastern scripture, the *Tantra-loka:* "Divine Grace leads the individual to the path of spiritual realization. It is the only cause

of Self-realization and is independent of human
effort."

The experience of Self-realization occurs
when the mind is concentrated to a fine laser-
point and focused in contemplation of God; but
this happens only by the power of the universal
Self, of God Himself. This is not a denial of
the efficacy of self-effort, but merely an assertion
that every effort or desire to remember Him,
every intensification of concentration on Him,
is instigated by Himself, for He is our own inner
Self, the inner Controller. It is He who inspires,
enacts, and consummates all our efforts.

Among the Christian mystics, we find
complete agreement on this issue; Saint Bernard
of Clairvaux, for example, says: "You would
not seek Him at all, O soul, nor love Him at all,
if you had not been first sought and first
loved." [5] And Meister Eckhart acknowledges:
"It is He that prays in us and not we ourselves."[6]
To which the Blessed Jan Ruysbroeck concurs:

> Contemplation places us in a purity
> and radiance which is far above our under-
> standing, ... and no one can attain to it
> by knowledge, by subtlety, or by any
> exercise whatsoever; but he whom God
> chooses to unite to Himself, and to illumine
> by Himself, he and no other can contemplate
> God. [7]

We find the same agreement among the Sufi
mystics, the Hindus and the Buddhists. It is
always so -- always. And though the attempt
is often made by charlatans to translate the
description of the mental state of the mystic at
the time of his experience of unity into a sort
of 'method' or 'scientific technique' for the
attainment of God, no one has ever claimed that
such a technique has actually produced the

advertised result. For, by themselves, the
practices of shallow breathing, fixed stares, and
cessation of thought, will never produce the
experience of unity. This experience comes
only by the Will of God. Nanak, the great
founder of the Sikh tradition, acknowledging
this truth, wrote:

> Liberation from bondage depends
> upon Thy Will; there is no one to
> gainsay it. Should a fool wish to,
> suffering will teach him wisdom. [8]

When He draws the mind to Himself, the
mind becomes still automatically. It is not
necessary to attempt to still the mind by
austere practices or artificial methods. The
body becomes still, the mind becomes still,
when the heart is yearning sincerely for Him
alone. Everything happens very naturally by
His Grace.

One begins to begrudge the mind any
thought save the thought directed to God. And
with the aim of centering the mind continually
on Him, one begins to sing His name in the inner
recesses of the mind. It doesn't matter what
name is used; Christians call Him, "Father,"
Muslims call Him "Allah," Jews call Him "Adonai,"
and Hindus call Him "Hari;" Love responds to
whatever name is called with love. To one who
loves, His name is nectar; it is like a cold drink
of water to a thirsty man. It is no discipline,
nor is it an austerity. It is the living of a
joyful life. It is the sweetness of peace; it is
the delight of delights.

Since there is really nothing else but that
infinite Being wherever one may look, as one
begins to sing the name of God, that awareness
dawns, and the bliss of recognizing one's own
Self both without and within begins to well up.
The more one sings His name, the more one revels

in that bliss, and the more clearly one perceives His continual presence. Inherent in that perception is all mercy, all right-judgement, all tenderness, all loving-kindness. It is the *natural devotion* by which a man's heart is transformed, and by which he becomes fit for the vision of God.

Everyone, sooner or later, comes to that period in their lives when they experience the Grace of God. It is experienced as an 'awakening of the soul', a prerequisite to the direct knowledge of God. This 'awakening' very often coincides with the hearing or reading of the words of someone who has had an especially profound experience of the Self, and who is able to communicate the understanding he has acquired. It seems that it is in this way, through our intellects, that God reaches to our hearts.

Speaking from my own experience, the moment I learned of the ultimate identity of man's self and the universal Self, a delicious joy arose in me coupled with a certainty that it was indeed true. I *felt* that inner Grace; I knew that I had found the truth of existence, and I rejoiced in that blissful knowledge! This, I believe, is a common experience, a universal symptom of the first flush of the soul's awakening to the Self. Sometimes this awakening is accompanied by thrills of joy that run up the spine into the head. Sometimes there are interior visions, either of saints or temples or simply of a golden light. But it is unmistakeable; it is truly an awakening of the soul, and is known and experienced as such.

It is clear that, as our destinies unfold, as the heavens tell the passing of our days, the focus of our awareness undergoes gradual changes. A decade ago, we sought quite different goals

from those which we seek at present; and yet
different objectives motivated us ten years
before that. These changes occur so gradually,
we scarcely notice that we have changed; yet
each new era in the unfolding of our destiny
has its own focus, its own learning experiences.
Eventually, each of us passes through a specific
period in our lives during which our understanding
is awakened to the Self, when we are most keenly
receptive to the awareness of God's presence and
Love. Years later, our ability to experience
that same sense of God's presence and Love may
wane; perhaps we shall pass into a period of more
mundane considerations during which we will
learn to carry the understandings which we
gained in those more ecstatic and spiritually
receptive moments into our daily lives, and to
remain obedient to that acquired wisdom.

The point I wish to make is that the time
of peak receptivity, the time of Grace, is short;
and should be cherished and utilized with care.
Once that unmistakeable awakening has occurred,
find some time to enjoy a period of solitude with
God. You will learn more in such moments than
in a thousand congregational lectures. Forge
your link with God, and He will lead you to Himself.
He will draw you to love Him, for He Himself is
that Love that has awakened in you as love for
God. He will draw you to seek Him in prayer and
in silent longing, for He is your own heart.
Follow, and you will reach Him. Draw near to
Him in the silence of the night and He will reveal
Himself to you as your very deepest Self, your
eternal Identity.

Do not imagine that a Guru, Master, or
Adept can be of any further help to you. Once
the teacher's words, inspired by his own vision
of Truth, have affected an awakening in you,
his work is done. Those who would bind you
to them as a disciple or servant in exchange for

their "grace" are frauds who seek only to milk
you to advance their own personal power, wealth
and prestige. Stay far away from them. They
will tell you that you need the Guru and his
special power to make progress in the spiritual
life; you do not. You need only God's Grace:
the Love of your own heart. *That* is the only
fee for entrance into the Kingdom of God.

Keep on loving Him, keep on trusting in
Him to guide you, and keep on praying to Him.
And when He puts it into your heart to know
Him, He will lift aside the veil, and reveal that,
all along, it was Him who prayed, who sought,
who sorrowed as you; and that, all along, it
was you who forever lives beyond all sorrow,
as God -- forever blissful, forever free.

*   *   *

APPENDIX

Two Songs

SONG ONE

Thou art Love, and I shall follow all Thy ways.
I shall have no care, for Love cares only to love.
I shall have no fear, for Love is fearless;
Nor shall I frighten any, for Love comes sweetly
                                    and meek.
I shall keep no violence within me, neither in
                        thought nor in deed,
For Love comes peacefully.
I shall bear no shield or sword, for the defense
                        of Love is love.
I shall seek Thee in the eyes of men, for love
                        seeks Thee always.
I shall keep silence before Thine enemies,
And lift to them Thy countenance, for all are
                        powerless before Thee.
I shall keep Thee in my heart with precious care,
Lest Thy light be extinguished by the winds;
For without Thy light, I am in darkness.
I shall go free in the world with Thee --
Free of all bondage to anything but Thee --
For Thou art my God, the sole Father of my
                                    being,
The sweet breath of Love that lives in my heart;
And I shall follow Thee, and live with Thee,
And lean on Thee till the end of my days.

SONG TWO

O my God, even this body is Thine own!
Though I call to Thee and seek Thee amidst
                              chaos,
Even I who seemed an unclean pitcher amidst
                              Thy waters --

Even I am Thine own.
Does a wave cease to be of the ocean?
Do the mountains and the gulfs cease to be of
                              the earth?

Or does a pebble cease to be stone?
How can I escape Thee?
Thou art even That which thinks of escape!
Even now, I speak the word, "Thou",
and create duality.
I love, and create hatred.
I am in peace, and am fashioning chaos.
Standing on the peak, I necessitate the depths.
But now, weeping and laughing are gone;
Night is become day.
Music and silence are heard as one;
My ears are all the universe.
All motion has ceased;
Everything continues.
Life and death no longer stand apart.
No I, no Thou;
No now, or then.
Unless I move, there is no stillness.
Nothing to lament, nothing to vanquish,
Nothing to pride oneself on;
All is accomplished in an instant.
All may now be told without effort.
Where is there a question?
Where is the temple?
Which the Imperishable, which the abode?

I am the pulse of the turtle;
I am the clanging bells of joy.
I bring the dust of blindness;
I am the fire of song.
I am in the clouds and in the gritty soil;
In pools of clear water my image is found.
I am the dust on the feet of the wretched,
The toothless beggars of every land.
I have given sweets that decay to those who
                                    crave them;
I have given my wealth unto the poor and lonely.
My hands are open -- nothing is concealed.

All things move together of one accord;
Assent is given throughout the universe
                        to every falling grain.
The Sun stirs the waters of my heart,
And the vapor of my love flies to the four
                        corners of the world;
The Moon stills me, and the cold darkness
                                is my bed.
I have but breathed, and everything is
                                rearranged
And set in order once again.
A million worlds begin and end in every breath,
And, in this breathing, all things are sustained.

*   *   *

NOTES

NOTES

ONE: THE EXPERIENCE OF UNITY

1. *Svetasvatara Upanishad:* 6; J. Mascaro, *The Upanishads*, p. 95.

2. *Mundaka Upanishad:* 3.1; Mascaro, *op. cit.*, p. 80.

3. *Katha Upanishad:* 5; Mascaro, *op. cit.*, p. 64.

4. Plotinus, *Enneads*, VI: 7.34, 36; VI: 9.5 to 9.11.

5. C. de B. Evans, *Eckhart*, Vol. I, p. 221.

6. R.B. Blackney, *Meister Eckhart, A Modern Translation;*

7. *Ibid.*, p. 206.

8. Aldous Huxley, *The Perennial Philosophy*, p. 12.

9. C. de B. Evans, *op. cit.*, Sermon XXI.

TWO: THE APPEARANCE OF DUALITY

1. Shankaracharya, *Atma Bodha*, 8.9

2. Philo Judaeus, *De Cherubim*, 27f.

3. John, *The Fourth Gospel of The New Testament*, 8:54.

4. *Ibid.*, 13:40.

5. *Ibid.*, 1:1.

6. William T. de Barry, *Sources of Indian Tradition*, p. 415.

7. A.E. Affifi, *The Mystical Philosophy of Muhyid Din-ibnul 'Arabi*, p. 21.

8. *Ibid.*, p. 11.

9. *Ibid.*, p. 11.

10. *Ibid.*, pp. 10-11.

11.   *Ibid.*, p. 21.

12.   Rom Landau, *The Philosophy of Ibn 'Arabi*, pp. 83-84.

13.   *Ibid.*, p. 83.

14.   de Barry, *op. cit.*, pp. 445-446.

15.   *Rig Veda*, X.129.

16.   *Isha Upanishad*, V.

17.   Mascaro, *op. cit.*, p. 89.

18.   *Ibid.*, p. 92.

19.   Swami Prabhavananda, trans., *Srimad Bhagavatam*, "The Wisdom Of God", p. 5.

20.   Swami Prabhavananda, trans., *Viveka-chudamani*, "The Crest-Jewel Of Discrimination", pp. 82-84.

21.   *Ibid.*, pp. 58-59.

22.   *Ibid.*, pp. 63-64.

23.   *Avatamsaka Sutra*, quoted by D.T. Suzuki, *op. cit.*, p. 268.

25.   *Pratyabijnahridayam*, I.1.

26.   Jnanehsvar, *Amritanubhav*, I; 13, 26-28, 10-12, 34-35, 39-40.

27.   R. Jastrow, *God And The Astronomers*. Intro.

THREE: THE PHYSICS OF UNITY

1.   A. de Riencourt, *The Eye Of Shiva*, pp. 169-170.

2.   L. de Broglie, *The Revolution In Physics*, p. 218.

3.   H. Pagels, *The Cosmic Code: Quantum Physics As The Language Of Nature*, p. 264.

4.   A. Einstein, quoted by M. Capek, *The Philosophical Impact Of Contemporary Physics*, p. 319.

5.   H. Pagels, *op. cit.*, p. 332.

6.   Jnaneshvar, *Changadev Pasashti*, IV.

7.   D. Bohm and B. Hiley, "On The Intuitive Understanding Of Non-Locality As Implied By Quantum Theory", *Foundations Of Physics*, Vol. V (1975); pp. 96, 102.

8.   Neils Bohr, quoted by G. Amaldi, *The Nature Of Matter*, p. 110.

9.   B. Hoffman, *The Strange Story Of The Quanta*, p. 179.

10.   G. Zukav, *The Dancing Wu Li Masters*, p. 28.

11.   M. Planck, *Where Is Science Going?*

12.   Baruch Spinoza, *Ethics*, II.48.

13.   *Ibid.*, I., App.

FOUR: THE PSYCHOLOGY OF UNITY

1.   Swami Vidyaranya, *Panchadashi*, 5.3.

2.   Werner Heisenberg, *Physics And Beyond*, p. 113.

3.   Shankaracharya, *Atma Bodha*, 18.

4.   *Ibid.*, 34.

5.   *Ibid.*, 37.

6.   *Mundaka Upanishad*, 3.2.

7.   Swami Prabhavananda (1947), *op. cit.*

8.   R. Hand, *Astrological Symbols*, p. 75.

9.   Plotinus, *Enneads*, II.3.6.

10. *Ibid.*, II.3.7.

11. Jnaneshvar, *Amritanubhav*, VII: 240, 135, 143, 144, 146, 163.

FIVE: THE WORSHIP OF UNITY

1. Jan Ruysbroeck, *The Sparkling Stone*, X.

2. Kabir, adapted from H.P. Shastri, *Indian Mystic Verse*, p. 49.

3. Ramakrishna, quoted by S. Nikhilananda, *The Gospel Of Ramakrishna;*

4. Swami Prabhavananda (1947), *op. cit.*, p. 131.

5. St. Bernard of Clairvaux, *On The Song Of Songs*, Sermon LXXXIV.4.

6. R.B. Blackney, *op. cit.*, p. 109.

7. Jan Ruysbroeck, *The Sparkling Stone*, IV.

8. Nanak, from Trilochan Singh, et. al., *Selections From The Sacred Writings Of The Sikhs*, p. 42.

BIBLIOGRAPHY

Affifi, A.E. *The Mystical Philosophy of Muhyid Din-ibnul 'Arabi,* Cambridge; AMS Press, 1939.

Amaldi, Ginestra *The Nature Of Matter,* Chicago; University of Chicago Press, 1966.

Hoffman, Banesh *The Strange Story Of The Quanta,* New York; Dover Publications, 1959.

Arberry, A.J. *Sufism: An Account of The Mystics of Islam,* London; Allen & Unwin, 1950.

Arnold, Edward V. *Roman Stoicism,* Freeport, N.H.; Books For Libraries Press, 1971.

Babbitt, Irving *The Dhammapada,* New York; Oxford University Press, 1936.

Barbour, Ian G. *Issues In Science And Religion,* Englewood Cliffs, N.J.; Prentice-Hall, 1966.

Barnett, Lincoln *The Universe And Dr. Einstein,* New York; Wm. Morrow & Co., 1948.

Blackney, R.B. *Meister Eckhart, A Modern Translation,* New York; Harper & Bros., 1941.

Bohm, David *Wholeness And The Implicate Order,* London; Routledge & Kegan Paul, 1980.
_____ *Causality And Chance In Modern Physics,* London; Routledge & Kegan Paul, 1957.

Bohr, Neils *Atomic Physics And Human Knowledge,* New York; Science Editions, 1961.

Calder, Nigel *The Key To The Universe,* London; British Broadcasting Corp., 1977.

Campbell, Joseph, ed. *Myths And Symbols In Indian Art And Civilization,* New York; Pantheon Books, 1963.

Capek, M. *The Philosophical Impact Of Contemorary Physics,* Princeton, N.J.; D. Van Nostrand, 1961.

Capra, Fritjof *The Tao Of Physics,* Boulder; Shambhala, 1975.

D'aygalliers, A.W. *Ruysbroeck, The Admirable,* New York; Kennikat Press, 1969.

de Barry, Wm. T., ed. *Sources Of Indian Tradition*, New York; Columbia Univ. Press, 1958.

de Broglie, Louis *The Revolution In Physics*, New York; Noonday Press, 1953.

De Marquette, J. *Introduction To Comparative Mysticism*, New York; Philosophical Library, 1949.

de Riencourt, Amaury *The Eye Of Shiva*, New York; Wm. Morrow & Co., 1981.

Drennen, D.A., ed. *A Modern Introduction To Metaphysics*, New YOrk; Free Press Of Glencoe, 1962.

Durant, Will *Ceasar And Christ*, New York; Simon & Schuster, 1944.

Gal-Or, Benjamin *Cosmology, Physics And Philosophy*, New York; Springer-Verlag, 1981.

Gamow, George *Thirty Years That Shook Physics*, New York; Doubleday & Co., 1966.

Guilleman, Victor *The Story Of Quantum Mechanics*, New York; Charles Scribner's Sons, 1968.

Hand, Robert *Astrological Symbols*, Para Research, Inc., Rockfort, Mass., 1980.

Heisenberg, Werner *Physics And Philosophy*, New York; Harper &Bros., 1958.

Huxley, Aldous *The Perennial Philosophy*, New York; World Publishing Co., 1944.

Hyman, A. & Walsh, J. *Philosophy In The Middle Ages*, New York; Harper & Row, 1967.

Inge, W.R. *Christian Mysticism*, New York; Meridian Books, 1950.

Isherwood, Christopher, ed. *Vedanta For The Western World*, Hollywood; Vedanta Press, 1946.

Jammer, Max *Concepts Of Force, A Study In The Foundations Of Dynamics*, New York; Harper Torchbooks, 1957.
_____ *The Philosophy Of Quantum Mechanics*, New York; John Wiley & Sons, 1974.

Jastrow, Robert *God And The Astronomers*,
New York; W.W. Norton & Co., 1978.

Jeans, Sir James *Physics And Philosophy*, Cambridge; Cambridge University Press, 1948.

Jnaneshvar *Jnaneshvari*, trans. by V.G. Pradhan,
(2 vols.), London; Allen & Unwin, 1969.

Jones, Rufus *The Flowering Of Mysticism*, New
York; Macmillan, 1939.

Kadlowbousky, E. & Palmer, G.E.H., trans.
The Philokalia, London; Faber & Faber,
1954.

Katsaros, T. & Kaplan, N. *The Western Mystical
Tradition, Vol. I*, New Haven; College &
University Press, 1969.

Kirk, K.E. *The Vision Of God*, New York; Harper
Torchbooks, 1966.

Landau, Rom *The Philosophy Of Ibn 'Arabi*,
London; Allen & Unwin, 1959.

Lao Tzu *The Way And Its Power*, trans. by Arthur
Waley, London; 1933.

Lindsay, Jack *Origins Of Astrology*, New York;
Barnes & Noble, Inc., 1971.

Ling, Trevor *The Buddha*, New York; Chas.
Scribner's Sons, 1973.

MacKenna, Stephen, trans. *Plotinus, The Enneads*,
London; Faber & Faber, 1956.

Magill, Frank N. & Mc Greal, I.P. *Masterpieces
Of Christian Literature*, New York; Harper
& Row, 1963.

Mahadevan, T.M.P. *Ramana Maharshi: The Sage
Of Arunachala*, London; Allen & Unwin, 1977.
_____ *Invitation To Indian Philosophy*, New Delhi;
Arnold Heinemann, 1974.

Mascaro, Juan, trans. *Bhagavad Gita*, Middlesex,
Penguin Books, 1962.
_____ *The Upanishads*, Middlesex; Penguin Books,
1965.

McIntosh, Christopher *The Astrologers And Their
Creed*, London; Hutchinson & Co., 1969.

Murchie, Guy *Music Of The Spheres*, New York;
Houghton Mifflin, 1961.

Nicholson, Reynold A. *The Mathnawi of Jalal-ud-din Rumi, (6 vols.)*, London; 1925.

Nikhilananda, Swami, trans. *The Gospel Of Ramakrishna*, New York; Ramakrishna-Vivekananda Center, 1942.

Otto, Rudolph *Mysticism East And West*, New York; Meridian Books, 1957.

Pagels, Heinz R. *The Cosmic Code: Quantum Physics As The Language Of Nature*, New York; simon & Schuster, 1982.

Petry, Ray C., ed. *Late Medieval Mysticism; Vol. XIII of The Library Of Christian Classics*, Philadelphia; Westminster Press, 1957.

Planck, Max *Where Is Science Going?*, London; Allen & Unwin, 1933.

Prabhavananda, Swami, trans. *Vivekachudamani by Shankaracharya*, Hollywood; Vedanta Press, 1947.
_____ *Srimad Bhagavatam, "The Wisdom Of God"*, Madras; Sri Ramakrishna Math, 1978.
_____ *The Spiritual Heritage Of India*, New York; Doubleday & Co., 1963.

Radhakrishnan, S. *Indian Philosophy*, London; Allen & Unwin, 1923.
_____ *Eastern Religions And Western Thought*, London; Allen & Unwin, 1939.

Ranade, R.D. *Pathway To God In Hindi Literature*, Bombay; Bharatiya Vidya Bhavan, 1959.

Schimmel, Annemarie *Mystical Dimensions Of Islam*, N.C.; University of North Carolina Press, 1975.

Shastri, H.P. *Indian Mystic Verse*, London; Shanti Sadan, 1941.
_____ *Panchadashi by Vidyaranya*, London; Shanti Sadan, 1965.

Singh, Trilochan, et al., eds. *Selections From The Sacred Writings Of The Sikhs*, London; Allen & Unwin, 1960.

Stace, W.T. *The Teaching Of The Mystics*,
New York; Mentor, 1969.
_____ *Mysticism And Philosophy*, New York;
J.B. Lippencott Co., 1960.
Suzuki, D.T. *Mysticism: Christian & Buddhist*,
New York; Harper & Bros., 1957.
_____ *Outlines Of Mahayana Buddhism*, New York;
Schocken Books, 1963.
Tagore, Rabindranath *One Hundred Poems Of
Kabir*, London; 1915.
Tauber, Gerald, ed. *Albert Einstein's Theory
Of General Relativity*, New York; Crown
Publishers, 1979.
Turnbull, Grace H., ed. *The Essence Of Plotinus*,
based on the translation of Stephen MacKenna,
New York; Oxford Univ. Press, 1934.
Underhill, Evelyn *Mysticism*, New York; E.P.
Dutton, 1961.
Vivekananda, Swami *Jnana Yoga*, New York;
Ramakrishna-Vivekananda Center, 1949.
Watts, Alan *The Supreme Identity*, New York;
Noonday Press, 1957.
_____ *The Two Hands Of God*, New York; Macmillan
Publishing Co., 1963.
Weinberg, Steven *The First Three Minutes*,
New York; Basic Books, 1977.
White, John, ed. *The Highest State Of Conscious-
ness*, New York; Doubleday Anchor, 1972.
Wolfson, Harry A. *Philo: Foundations Of Religious
Philosophy In Judaism, Christianity, and
Islam (2 vols.)*, Cambridge, Harvard Univ.
Press, 1947.
_____ *The Philosophy Of The Church Fathers*,
Cambridge; Harvard Univ. Press, 1970.
Zolar *The History Of Astrology*, New York;
Arco Publishing Co., 1972.
Zukav, Gary *The Dancing Wu Li Masters*, New
York; Bantam Books, 1979.

Stace, W.T. The Teachings Of The Mystics,
    New York: Mentor, 1960.

_____. Mysticism And Philosophy, New York:
    J.B. Lippencott Co., 1960?

Suzuki, D.T. Buddhism, Christian & Buddhist
    New York: Harper & Bros., 1957.

_____. Outlines Of Mahayana Buddhism, New York:
    Schocken Books, 1963.

Tagore, Rabindranath. Collected Poems Of
    Rabindranath, 1911.

Stauffer, Donald, ed. Albert Einstein's Theory
    Of General Relativity, New York: Crown
    Publishers, 1979.

Turnbull, Grace H., ed. The Essence Of Plotinus,
    based on the translation of Stephen MacKenna,
    New York: Oxford Univ. Press, 1934.

Underhill, Evelyn, Mysticism, New York: E.P.
    Dutton, 1961.

Vivekananda, S. and Isherwood, New York:
    Ramakrishna-Vivekananda Center, 1948.

Watts, Alan The Supreme Identity, New York:
    Noonday Press, 1957.

_____. Two Hands Of God, New York: Collier Macmillan
    Publishers Co., 1963.

Weinberg, Steven. The First Three Minutes,
    New York: Basic Books, 1977.

White, John, ed. The Highest State Of Consciousness,
    New York: Doubleday Anchor, 1972.

Wolfson, Harry A. The Philosophy Of The Church
    Fathers, in Judaism, Christianity, and
    Islam (2 vols.), Cambridge, Harvard Univ.
    Press, 1947.

_____. The Philosophy Of The Church Fathers,
    Cambridge, Harvard Univ. Press, 1976.

Wolfe, The History Of Astronomy, New York:
    Harper & Row Co., 1973.

Zukav, Gary The Dancing Wu Li Masters, New
    York: Bantam Books, 1979.

INDEX

ABSOLUTE, THE 45, 59, 90, 133
acharya 46
adrasteia 107
Akbar, king 42
as-Bastami, Abu Yazid 39
al-Hallaj, Mansur 39, 134
al-Ghazali 7
Arjuna 52
astrologers 108, 109, 112, 117
Astrology 108, 109
Atman 51
Attar, Fraid-ud-din 40
Aurangzeb 42
Avatamsaka Sutra 56
awakening, spiritual 3, 5, 35, 141, 142
awareness, pure 32

BABYLON 109
Being 5, 33, 47, 49, 94, 137
Bhagavad Gita 46, 52
bhaktas 134, 135, 137
bhakti 133
Bliss, absolute 60, 107
body, the 23, 33, 49, 68, 104, 123
Bohm, David 81
Bohr, Neils 70, 86, 87, 89, 101
Brahma Sutras 47
Brahman 45, 47, 48, 49, 50, 53, 55, 57, 97, 107
brahmins 55
Buddha, the 12, 31, 46, 54-56
Buddhism 54-56
Buddhist saints 7, 12, 139

Unity
    experience of 4, 9, 10, 11, 12, 18, 31,
        39, 41, 53, 107, 112, 121, 137, 140
    philosophy of 32, 40, 44, 47
    the 10, 31, 39, 40, 41, 127
universe, the 21, 26, 40, 45, 58, 59, 83, 93
    mother of 30
University of California 7
Upanishad,
    Isha 45
    Katha 8
    Mundaka 8, 106
    Svetasvatara 8, 45, 46
Upanishads, the 3, 7, 8, 33, 42, 44, 47, 55,
        106

VEDANTA 3, 4, 44-50
Vedanta For The Western World 3
Vedas, the 3, 44, 55
Vedic sages 12
Vidyaranya, Swami 7
vision, mystical 4, 13, 34
Vivekachudamani 47, 107, 132, 138
Void, the 44, 60
vrittis 101

WAVES 19, 21, 31, 32, 43
West, the 33, 34
    seers of 8
Western culture 8
Whole,
    the unbroken 22, 48, 68, 76, 77, 80, 81,
        82, 94, 120, 127
    constancy of the 77, 78, 79
Will,
    divine 34
    free 59, 87, 92, 93, 94, 121, 122, 123
    power of 34, 45, 57, 59, 120

Like to send a copy of this book to a friend? Additional copies of THE SUPREME SELF may be ordered directly from the publisher at the list price of $19.95, plus postage. Use the coupon below.

Also

Look for Swami Abhayananda's newest book to be released soon: JNANESHVAR — The Life And Works Of The Celebrated 13th Century Indian Mystic-Poet. The dramatic, never-before-told story of one of the world's most revered saints and beloved poets. With selections from his most beautiful and inspiring works.

☐ Please send me ____ copies of THE SUPREME SELF, at $19.95 per copy, plus postage.* I am enclosing check ( ) money order ( ) for $ _____

☐ Please inform me when Swami Abhayananda's new book, JNANESHVAR, becomes available.

_____
name

_____
address

_____
city   state   zip

Make checks payable to: ATMA BOOKS, P.O. Box 432, Fallsburg, NY 12733

* Postage: $1.00 for first book, 25¢ for each additional book.

Like to send a copy of this book
to a friend?
Additional copies of THE SUPREME SELF
may be ordered directly from the publisher at
the list price of $9.95, plus postage. Use the
coupon below.

- Also -
Look for Swami Abhayananda's newest book
to be released soon: *JNANESHVAR -- The Life
And Works Of The Celebrated 13th Century Indian
Mystic-Poet*. The dramatic, never-before-told
story of one of the world's most revered saints
and beloved poets. With selections from his
most beautiful and inspiring works.

- -

[ ] Please send me _____ copies of
THE SUPREME SELF, at $9.95 per copy,
plus postage.* I am enclosing check ( )
money order ( ) for $_____.

[ ] Please inform me when Swami Abnayananda's
new book, *JNANESHVAR*, becomes available.

_____
name

_____
address

_____
city   state   zip

Make checks payable to: ATMA BOOKS,
P.O. Box 432, Fallsburg, NY 12733

* *Postage: $1.00 for first book, 25¢ for
each additional book.*